Trial By Fire

By Susan E. Hilliard

Illustrated by Ned O.

STANDARD PUBLISHING
Cincinnati, Ohio   24-03985

Library of Congress Cataloging-in-Publication Data
Hilliard, Susan E.
  Trial by fire/Susan E. Hillard.
    p. cm.—(Decide your own adventure)
  Summary: The reader makes choices about the unfolding
of the life of Abraham.
  ISBN 0-87403-725-5
  1. Abraham (Biblical patriarch—Juvenile literature. 2.
Bible. O.T. Genesis—Biography—Juvenile literature. 3. Plot-
your-own stories. [1. Abraham (Biblical patriarch) 2. Bible
stories—O.T. 3. Plot-your-own stories.] I. Title. II. Series:
Hilliard, Susan E. Decide your own adventure.
BS580.A3H53 1990
222',11092—dc20   90-33964
                                                        CIP
                                                         AC

Edited by Teresa C. Hayes

Attention, Reader!

You cannot read this book as you would any other. You are embarking upon a very special journey. On this journey, you will travel in a chariot of fire in order to discover the answer to a quest that will soon be given to you. During your quest, you will sometimes be allowed to choose between alternate events and/or times. When you make your decision, the chariot will take you swiftly to the place of your choice.

After you have found the chariot, the clothes you will wear, and the rules for travel, your next step is to look for two scrolls of parchment in the chariot. The first is your quest, and the second parchment is a vital archive of historical facts that can aid you in making the right choice at the proper time.

And now, begin your adventure!

The Chariot

A chariot of fire stands before you. The chariot seems solid, although it appears to be completely in flames. Your heart thudding, you step closer and notice that the fire is not hot—only pleasantly warm. Through the shimmering flames you see a beautiful horse hitched to the chariot, standing patiently. The beast seems so serene that the violent hammering of your heart calms down, and you step hesitantly into the chariot. Nothing happens. You are surrounded by flames, yet nothing is burning. You step farther into the chariot and notice a plain wooden box on the floor. Upon the box is written "Rules for Travel." You open the box.

On the inside of the lid, you read....

Rules for Travel

You must follow these rules on your journey. If you do not, the chariot will return you to the present, and you will never be able to complete your quest.

 I. You may not change history in any way—you are only an observer.

 II. You may choose only from the alternatives that you are given.

 III. You may not bring twentieth-century customs, clothing, or equipment with you. Tell no one you may meet of your journey.

 IV. You may not bring any souvenirs of your journey home with you.

You will find that language differences will not be a problem for you—you will automatically think and speak in the language of your host time and place.

Inside the box is a brightly-colored cloth. You pull it out eagerly, shaking out fold after fold. As you hold it up, you see that it is a tunic with vertical stripes creating a bright pattern of blues, golds, and reds. It appears to cover one shoulder only, forming a short sleeve and leaving the other shoulder uncovered.

Swiftly, you remove your twentieth-century clothing and pull the tunic over your head. You are relieved that it is shorter than ankle-length — you have a feeling it would take you some time to learn not to become tangled in a tunic that reached your ankles!

Impatiently, the hooves of the snowy steed paw the ground; a thrill of excitement races down your spine—you are also eager to begin! Tossing your twentieth-century clothes into the bushes, you begin to search the confines of the chariot for the quest and the archives.

Dropping to your knees, your fingers grope into the dark forward corners of the small chariot. At last—you touch something that feels like two cylinders of paper. Eagerly, you draw them out and find that they are two scrolls. Anxious to discover your quest, you unroll the smaller scroll and read....

The Quest

You are instructed to go to the time of Abram, to discover why his name was changed to Abraham, and why that name change is important to us today.

You remember that Abraham is sometimes called the "Father of the Faithful," by both Jews and Christians. You also remember that God asked Abraham to sacrifice his only son. You wonder how loving a father Abraham could have been, to have been willing to do such a thing. And why on earth would a simple name change be so important to anyone?

Puzzled, you unroll the larger scroll, and glance through it swiftly. On this scroll, you find written....

Archives

I. Both Jews and Arabs have an age-old tradition that Enoch, who lived long before Abram, invented writing—and that his "books" (clay tablets) remained after he was taken to Heaven. However, modern scholars used to believe that there was no writing during Abram's time, so they felt that his story was recorded long after it actually occurred, placing the account in the "folk tale" category. Archaeologists have since discovered that writing was actually well-developed before 3,000 B.C.—at least 1,000 years before Abram lived.

II. Abram was born in Ur of the Chaldees, about twelve miles north of the traditional location of the Garden of Eden. During Abram's time (approximately 2,000 B.C.), Ur was a thriving and sophisticated city. The main god of Ur was Nannar, the moon god. His wife was called Ningal, the moon goddess. A massive ziggurat in their honor was located inside the city walls of Ur. Archaeologists have uncovered fabulous royal tombs at Ur, dating before the time of Abram.

III. Inscriptions found on the earliest clay tablets tell us that mankind's first religion was the worship of one God. From that point, most cultures degenerated into polytheism—worship of many gods. The overwhelming evidence discovered by researchers suggests that almost all tribes have a memory in their literature of a "High God" who is our Creator.

IV. Married couples who did not have children were thought to be woefully unfortunate. Many children—especially sons—were a sign of blessing and status. Abram and Sarai were married many years before Isaac was born and they probably suffered many taunts about their childlessness.

V. A person's name was very important in the Middle East. Names always had special meanings, and were supposed to describe an aspect of the bearer's character. Abram meant "exalted father"—quite a burden for a man with no children at all.

VI. A covenant was a very serious and binding agreement between two parties. To break a covenant was punishable by death.

VII. Archaeologists tell us that the Sodom and Gomorrah area was no longer populated after about 1900 B.C., evidently due to something catastrophic that occurred there. The Dead Sea now covers the land where the cities once were.

You decide you had better keep this scroll with you, for you have a feeling that you might need to read it more carefully. You tuck it into your sash, where the folds of the tunic hide it completely.

You pick up the leather reins and hold them loosely in your hands. Now what? You pull the smooth leather taut and suddenly....

(At the Beginning)

A fresh breeze stirs your tunic as you look down from the roof of a two-story house to dew-drenched fields below. A rooster crows in the distance and a flaming sun bursts over the eastern horizon. You hear the sound of voices and footsteps coming up the stairs to the roof and, not knowing what to expect, you crouch down behind some tall water jars. Two men step out onto the roof. The age of the first man is hard to determine. Although his hair is graying and his face looks as though it has seen many years, he is powerfully built and full of vigor. The man following him is, without a doubt, very old.

"Master," the old man quavers as he bows before the other, "why must you go from this home that you and your father have built?"

The younger man smiles gently, stooping to lift the old man to his feet. "You know I must go, Hiram. The Lord God has told me that I must go to a land which He will show me—how could I refuse to obey?"

Tears trickle down the leathery old cheeks. "Master Abram," he pleads, "I have known you since you were a baby. You grew up in Ur and you have grown wealthy beyond imagination here in Haran. You have gold and silver treasures, great herds of oxen and flocks of sheep, and many manservants and maidservants accountable to you. *Why* must you leave the home where God has so richly blessed you?"

Abram places his arm around the old servant.

"When the Lord God speaks, Hiram, we must obey.
I will go where He leads me."

Hiram shakes his head stubbornly. "Then you are
set on this?" he asks tearfully. "You will truly leave
so soon after your father's death on this journey
into the unknown?" His voice rises in feeble rage,

but Abram only smiles tenderly. "You will take all your family and servants into the wilderness? How will you know when you have reached this land that God has promised to you?"

"I will take my wife, and my herds and flocks, and as many servants as we will need to care for us and the animals," he answers softly, "and I will take my brother's son, Lot. How could I leave him behind? Lot is like my own son now, since his father died." Abram pauses and looks out into the desert beyond.

"No, I do not know where I am going—I know only that I must go where my Lord leads me!"

Hiram throws his arms around Abram. "Then take me with you, my master!" he pleads. "If you must go, then I will follow!"

"No, my faithful old friend," answers Abram gently. "This journey will be too much for you. I would not have you suffer; that is why I have provided for you to stay in this house where you have tended me so carefully for the seventy-five years of my life. You have served my father and me well—finish your days here, in peace, in the city that you love."

"But what will happen?" Hiram wails in anguish. "Where will you go?"

"My caravan will set off in the direction of Canaan," replies Abram firmly. "But where we will end up, I do not know."

Abram's voice is dreamy and his eyes far away as he continues. "I go where the Lord leads me, for it is He who has promised to give me a land. The Lord God has blessed me and has said that in me all the families of the earth will be blessed." His voice gathers strength as he continues, "The journey may take my entire life—I may struggle with bleeding feet in the high mountains, my tongue may swell with burning thirst in the heat of the desert—what difference does it make where I go, as long as I follow where my Maker leads?"

You watch Abram's radiant face in awe, for you cannot understand the depth of faith he has to leave his home to begin a journey into the unknown. And you are astonished to learn that he is seventy-five years old! He is beginning this great adventure at a time when most men you know would be retiring to a life of ease!

Abram smiles gently at Hiram. "Everything will be all right, dear friend. Trust in the Lord, and be at peace."

Leaping flames suddenly blot the scene from your sight and you find to your surprise that you are once more in the chariot, behind the magnificent steed. Chills race down your spine as the flames surround you, and a musical voice, seeming to come from the steed itself, splinters the silence.

"Now it is time for your first decision," says the voice. "You may go a little forward in time to see Abram leave Haran, or you may go farther forward to see the battle of the nine kings. Which will you choose?"

Eager to begin your quest in earnest, you take the cool leather reins in your hands and make your decision.

If you decide to go to the battle of nine kings, go to page 54.

If you decide to see Abram leave Haran, go to page 30.

(You Have Decided to Go Back to Ur)

The loud bray of a donkey startles you. You find yourself in a throng of people in the middle of a busy thoroughfare. The sky overhead is deep azure, and the sun warms your back. A light breeze lifts your hair, and birds circle lazily overhead.

The babble of voices everywhere mixing with the braying of donkeys creates a confusing din. You are jostled roughly from behind and whirl around to confront the sneering mouth of a camel. Hastily you step to one side, as the heavily-loaded animal lumbers past you. Through the dense crowd you glimpse a sparkle of water. Making your way through the throng you finally see a broad river.

On the other side of the river, you are astonished to see city walls rising sharply from the fertile plain. Yellow brick walls rise to wide ramparts, where soldiers march vigilantly, their close-fitting helmets sparkling in the sun. You see what almost looks like a mountain inside the city walls, but the shimmer of heat waves makes a clear view impossible. Suddenly, a heavily-laden donkey just ahead of you stops dead in his tracks, spilling a heavy sack from the baskets hanging over either side of his back. You jump back, but not fast enough to avoid the sack— which lands squarely on your foot. You wince in pain and stoop to pick up the bulging skin bag. By the time you have hoisted it up to your shoulder, the donkey has surged through the crowd, over the bridge, and is just disappearing through the wide arched gate in the city wall. Hurrying to return the bag to its owner, you also enter the city.

Narrow streets wander haphazardly in every direction, twisting between two-story houses built flush with the streets. *I expected a much more primitive city*, you realize in surprise. You break into a run — not easy in an elbow-to-elbow crowd — as you see the donkey disappearing around a sharp bend just ahead.

"Hey!" you shout. "You lost a sack!" The man at the donkey's head turns swiftly, his eyes scanning the contents of the baskets on the animal's back. His deeply-tanned face crinkles into a broad smile as you stumble to a stop beside him.

"Many thanks, young stranger," the man says pleasantly. "It would not do to short-change the god with my offering!"

"I am happy to have helped," you answer politely. One swift glance at this man rids your mind of the idea that the people of Abram's time were practically cave men — his face is intelligent and sophisticated. The man's tunic is plain, but an intricately-carved dagger is sheathed at his waist. His crisply-curled black beard glistens with a sweet-smelling oil, and a silver armband flashes on his muscular upper arm.

You realize that you have been staring and flush in embarrassment. The man's eyes twinkle as he places a friendly arm on your shoulder.

"Come, my young helper. Would you like to go to the temple with me?" he asks.

"Yes, sir!" you answer immediately. He chuckles as you fall into step beside him, the donkey plodding along behind. Throngs of people jostle you as

you follow the winding path between the houses for what seems like miles. At last, the houses end at the edge of a broad canal that cuts directly in front of you. A narrow stone bridge spans the canal.

"Is this a river?" you ask your companion. He stares at you curiously. "Have you never been inside the city before?" he asks in surprise. You shake your head.

The man smiles proudly. "Ur is a magnificent city—the gods are kind to us. No, that is a canal that links our two harbors!"

"Two?" you ask in surprise.

He nods vigorously. "Marvelous, is it not? We have merchants from countries far away trading their goods for ours."

As you come around a corner, you suddenly stop in astonishment, your mouth agape. A huge, stepped pyramid towers into the sky, its bottom level alone about fifty feet high. Your companion chuckles as he propels you forward again. Now you and he are skirting the wall that surrounds the magnificent structure.

You stare in astonishment at the pyramid— each level is smaller than the one beneath it, and each is filled with palms trees and flowers growing in riotous profusion.

"What is that?" you gasp.

"That is our shrine to the moon god, Nannar. It is called a ziggurat. Nannar and his wife, Ningal, keep our city strong and prosperous," he answers.

At last, you and your companion find a door in the high wall surrounding the ziggurat. Clean-shaven priests scurry busily within the vast enclosure. Your companion turns to you with a smile.

"Well, youngster—what would you like to do? Would you like to accompany me inside to take my offering to the priests? Or would you like to wander about the city a bit? I should not be inside too long, and would be glad to have your company again on the way home."

Dazed by what you have seen so far, you find it difficult to think clearly. What should you do?

If you decide to go inside the temple, go to page 27.

If you decide to wander around Ur, go to page 21.

(You Have Decided to Wander Around Ur)

"I think I'll just wander around a little," you answer. Your companion nods, smiling, and moves briskly toward the temple, leading the donkey behind him.

You look curiously at the massive ziggurat. Two huge staircases, flush with the front, lead up to the vaulted brick archways of the second story. Yet another staircase is at right angles to the front, and leads directly into the arch. Priests hurry up and down the stairs—looking much like busy ants on the enormous structure.

A crowd of people surges past you and you are carried along with them inside the temple walls. Wails of grief erupt from someone in the crowd and you scan the faces curiously. Suddenly, you trip and fall heavily to the ground.

"Here! Pick that up, idiot! And stay on your feet!" an unpleasant voice hisses in your ear. Dazed, you find yourself staring into eyes glittering with malice. "Do you want to find yourself on your knees for eternity?"

The man boxes your ears violently—your eyes water involuntarily at the unexpected pain. You grab the huge bow at your feet that the man is pointing to—that must have been what tripped you. Scrambling to your feet, you find your arm clutched in a crushing grip.

Without a word, the man marches you along with the group. The faces around you are sorrowful. At the head of the procession you catch a glimpse of a bier borne on men's shoulders. *I'm in the middle of a funeral procession!* you think uncomfortably. You look swiftly around, hoping for a way to escape.

"You'll not get away until I let you," growls the man menacingly, his hand still tight on your arm. Relentlessly he pushes you down a steep flight of steps — the bier has reached the bottom already.

The funeral procession crosses several yards of hard-packed earth, then descends yet another stairway. As you look around, you see that this area has many levels, each with its own stairway and each floored with dirt. At last the crowd stops, and the bier is carried down a slope into the earth. A hush falls on those present, and you wait uneasily.

Four men return, the bier empty now of its occupant. One man, his arms laden with spear, shield, golden cups and bowls, and what looks like a gaming board, stumbles down the ramp.

"Now, young mongrel!" your captor's voice says harshly, "Take the bow down — the servant will tell you where to place it."

Your heart thudding, you walk slowly into the

earth—from sunlight and life into darkness and death. At last the slope evens out. In the dimness you see the body of a soldier curled up on his side peacefully, as if in sleep. *This isn't so bad,* you think in relief. You peer curiously through the shadows for the servant. He is busily arranging cups and bowls within easy reach of the man who will never again need them.

An intricate, close-fitting gold helmet gleams dully in the twilight of the earth, protecting the head of the dead soldier.

"Here is the bow," you squeak, startled at the sound of your own voice. "Where do you want me to put it?"

The servant turns huge, frightened eyes toward you, and takes the bow with shaking hands. *What in the world is he so afraid of?* you wonder.

"Are you to stay to serve my master, too?" the servant asks in a quivering voice.

Your scalp prickles as goose-bumps crawl up your spine. "What do you mean, 'stay'?" you ask, your voice cracking.

"Stay to serve the master in eternity," he explains. "Do you think that it will hurt to die? Do you think it will be quick?"

Horrified, you respond swiftly, "No way! I'm not going to die here—and you don't have to either!"

The servant's cold, thin fingers close around your wrist in a desperate grasp. "But of course I have to," he quavers miserably. "It is my place to serve him in death, as well as in life. They will bury me alive if I don't drink the cup!"

He wrenches himself away from you, and sinks to his knees at the feet of the dead soldier. Taking a flask from the folds of his tunic, he tears out the stopper. You leap toward him, horrified, your hands reaching for the flask. But before you can grab it, he tilts his head back and drains the flask of its contents.

"NO!" you shriek in protest.

Your limbs feel numb with horror and revulsion as you stoop to pick up the empty vial. There is a roaring in your ears, and you see as if from a great distance that beads of sweat are forming on the pale forehead of the dying man.

"Go!" he gasps, the muscles in his face straining with the effort. "Quickly!"

Your legs feel like wood, but you force them to move up the ramp—you gain strength as you catch sight of the funeral crowd at the top. Your hands stretch out in front of you—for no one must stop you from leaving this evil place. All you can see is a blur of faces as you break into a desperate run.

The sun shines warmly down on the city of Ur as you race out of the ziggurat enclosure and into the street beyond. No one will *ever* be able to tell you that the worship of pagan gods is harmless!

The street disappears in the clean white flames of the chariot. Your chest aches and you sink gratefully back against the side of the chariot.

"What a horrible place!" you explode.

"Yes, little one—a city without God is a terrible place to be," replies the steed softly. "But now it is time for you to see Abram's arrival in Bethel."

"Where?" you ask blankly.

The steed's musical laughter sparkles in the air. "Abram's journey from the comfortable city life in Haran was long and difficult, my friend," the steed replies. "First, he went to Shechem, where he built an altar to the Lord. Then, after a time, he went south to Bethel."

Wow! you think admiringly. *Moving around with all those cattle and people couldn't have been easy!* You take the reins in your hands and wait.

Go to page 33.

(You Have Decided
 to Go Inside the Temple)

"I think I'll stay with you for a bit," you answer hesitantly.

"Good!" he says with a smile. "No one should visit Ur without a close look at our marvelous tower!"

You curiously inspect the massive ziggurat. Two huge staircases, flush with the front, lead up to the vaulted brick archways of the second story. Yet another staircase is at right angles to the front, and leads directly into the arch. Priests hurry up and down the stairs—looking much like busy ants on the enormous structure.

You shiver a little as you and your companion step into the shadow of the ziggurat of Ur.

"Is the tower very old?" you ask curiously.

"Ah!" the man sighs. "Yes and no, my friend. Our king, Ur-Nammu, has rebuilt the ziggurat in Babylon, as well as this one." He casts an uneasy glance over his shoulder, his voice sinking to a whisper. "It is said that the first building of the illustrious tower in Babylon offended the gods. In one night they threw down what the people had built, and made it impossible for them to rebuild the temple!"

"How did they do that?" you ask.

"The gods caused everyone to speak in strange languages, so that the workmen could not understand each other! And because they could not communicate with everyone, people divided into groups where they could understand each other

and scattered to points all over the earth!" he finishes, shuddering.

He is talking about the tower of Babel, you think in excitement. *And it was not the work of "the gods," it was the work of God!* You calculate swiftly that if Abram lived about four hundred years after the flood, and if the tower of Babel confusion took place one hundred years after the flood, then only about three hundred years have passed from the confusion of languages until now!

"We will speak no more of this," your companion says firmly. "Come! I must find a priest to take my offering to Nannar."

A priest erupts briskly from a small doorway in the base of the tower. He eyes the baskets on the donkey's back with a business-like air, and asks abruptly, "Your offerings?" Your companion nods, and the priest claps his hands imperiously. "Excel-

lent!" he says as several slaves hurry out of the doorway and begin unloading the bulging baskets. "If you will follow me, we will take a count of what you have brought to Nannar this day."

Your companion follows the priest into the doorway. Hesitating, you realize that you feel uncomfortable about entering the ziggurat. Suddenly, the shimmering white flames of the chariot surround you. Gratefully, you take the reins in your hands.

"You have no decision to make this time, young friend," says the steed quietly. "I take you now to Abram's arrival in Bethel."

You marvel that Abram remained faithful to the Lord while living in a city that seems completely absorbed in pagan worship *It will be good to see Abram again,* you think happily.

Go to page 33.

(You Have Decided to See Abram Leave Haran)

Blinking in brilliant sunshine, you find your-self outside tall city walls on a wide, dusty road that is jam-packed with jostling people and ani-mals. Above the excited babble of the crowd, merchants compete to sell their wares. Beehive-shaped brick houses crowd close around the city walls, and you stare at them in wonder.

You pick your way through the throng toward the city of Haran, listening to voices raised in excitement as the shoppers barter. Scanning the crowd absently, you see Abram's kind, honest face—and you elbow your way eagerly toward him. He stops suddenly, as a merchant lunges out to bar his path.

"Come, friend," pleads the merchant, "surely you do not wish to leave this fair city without purchasing teraphim, to aid you in your travels?"

Abram shakes his head emphatically. "I have no need of images of dead ancestors, friend," he replies firmly.

The merchant dives into his overflowing pack. "I understand perfectly!" he cries gleefully. "You are a wise man. Here is something that I know will please you." He thrusts a small, gleaming statue toward Abram. "Is this not a wonderful likeness of the beautiful goddess Ishtar? Your lovely wife surely will wish to have this!" he adds, leering at Sarai. "May the goddess Ishtar give you many children, my lady!"

Abram's eyes flash dangerously. "Away with you!" he says angrily. "I will have no idols of any kind in my keeping. Ply your wares somewhere else, merchant!"

The man's cheeks flush angrily. "Your father, Terah, was not too haughty to buy my wares, Abram! And he did well for himself in this city." His voice rises to a shriek, "You're in such a hurry to leave, you're hardly waiting until your father's body is cold! Aren't you *clever*, Abram, to follow the voice of a God who leads you out of prosperity into the wilderness!" Angrily, the merchant turns away from Abram.

Abram turns to a boy at his elbow and says gently, "Come, Lot—look once more upon the city, and we must be off."

Lot looks longingly at the bustling city, then turns reluctantly to follow Abram and Sarai. Servants follow behind, leading a flock of sheep and some donkeys laden with bulging baskets.

"But where are we going, Uncle?" the boy protests.

Patiently, Abram puts an arm about the boy's shoulders. "I have told you many times, my nephew," Abram sighs wearily. "The Lord will show us the land. You know well the promise He made to me."

Lot's lips curl scornfully as he shakes off his uncle's arm. "I know," he mutters. "He will give you a land, make your name great, and in you all the families of the earth will be blessed. I just don't see why He can't do all that right here!"

A frown creases Abram's brow, but it fades as he looks kindly at the boy. "You will see, Lot. It is better to follow the Lord God into the wilderness, than to prosper out of His will. You will see!" Abram tousles Lot's hair affectionately. "Now the great adventure really begins!"

In spite of himself, Lot's eyes sparkle with excitement as the journey into the unknown begins. Their faces fade as you are enfolded in shining, leaping flames.

"Here is your choice," chimes the musical voice. "You may go to Ur, the home of Abram's youth, to learn more about that city, or you may see Abram's arrival in Bethel."

Puzzling over which might help you more, you make your choice.

If you decide to go to Ur, go to page 16.

If you decide to see Abram's arrival in Bethel, go to page 33.

(You Have Come to See Abram's Arrival in Bethel)

Gusts of wind tear at your tunic as you find yourself near the summit of a low mountain. Sheep and goats dot the slopes all around you, grazing contentedly. Away to the east you see the remains of a city, its ruined rubble now home only to the birds that soar overhead.

"Here, youngster!" calls a cheerful voice. "As long as you are here, you may as well be useful!"

You turn in the direction of the voice, to see a man lifting a flattened boulder onto a low mound of similar rocks. He straightens, wiping the sweat from his brow with a bronzed forearm.

"Bring me that rock at your feet, will you?" he calls.

Dislodging the rock from the grass and soil that anchor it, you toil up the summit with the boulder. The man scrutinizes it carefully, then nods in satisfaction.

"This will do nicely," he says with a smile. He brushes the dirt from the rock, and places it atop the pile of rocks.

"What are you building?" you ask politely.

"I am building an altar to the Lord," he responds quietly. "Although," he adds, his eyes twinkling, "my wife probably thinks I would be of more use down there!" he says, pointing down the slope of the mountain.

Your eyes follow his pointing hand, and you see tents being set up on a flattened portion of the mountainside. A woman's voice rises in a wail, as a gust of wind tears at the largest tent, sending it billowing up the slope.

The man's shoulders shake with amusement. "Sarai will keep them hopping," he laughs. "My wife can organize the pitching of the tents with no help from me!"

"Abram?" you ask slowly, "Why are you building an altar here?"

Abram's eyes look dreamily into the distance as he answers, "Because, my friend, the Lord has promised this land to my descendants. How could I *not* build an altar to honor Him?"

Putting an arm around your shoulder, Abram points to the ruined city in the east. "Do you see the ruins of Ai?" he asks softly. "Even the name means 'heap.' Perhaps if the inhabitants had not worshiped false gods, the city would still be prospering today."

He gives your shoulders a brief pat, and glances down at the encampment bustling with activity. "I will finish the altar before I do anything else," he says firmly.

Abram turns back to his work, and you see the chariot of fire shimmering just over the crest of the mountain. You walk swiftly toward it and climb thoughtfully in.

The steed's voice pierces the throbbing silence of the flames. "Now for your choice. I shall take you a little forward in time, to Egypt."

"Egypt?" you ask curiously. "Did Abram go there?"

"Yes, for he found famine in Canaan shortly after his arrival," replies the voice. "So he journeyed on to Egypt. Would you choose to be with Abram's household in Egypt, or in the palace of the pharaoh?"

Excitement quickens your pulse at the idea of seeing a real pharaoh's palace! On the other hand, staying with Abram might help you more. You ponder a moment, then make your decision.

If you decide to be with the pharaoh in Egypt, go to page 41.

If you decide to be with Abram in Egypt, go to page 36.

(You Have Decided to Be With Abram in Egypt)

You blink in the blinding sunshine glaring off the surface of a river slowly winding its way amidst swaying palm trees. High-prowed boats move lazily on the water, and men at the river's edge are drawing in huge nets laden with fish.

Three massive pyramids tower into the sky some distance away. You are surprised, for you hadn't realized that the pyramids were so ancient. Goat-skin tents stretch out in every direction on this side of the river, while on the opposite side you can see one-story houses of brick set back from the water.

A child scurries past you, almost knocking you over in his haste. "Abram!" he cries excitedly. "Pharaoh wants to see you! His servant is on his way here right now!"

A tall, broad-shouldered man steps from the largest tent. He is clad in a patterned tunic and a thick roll of cloth encircles his head—almost like a twentieth-century sweat-band, you decide. You remember that Abram is more than seventy-five years old, and you are astonished at his appearance—although his face is lined, his body is in the condition of a man in the prime of life, and his hair and beard are barely marked with gray.

The child tumbles into Abram, who sweeps him high overhead. Giggling, the child continues, "Really! The servant told me so. See? Here he comes!" Your eyes are drawn to a short, dark-skinned Egyptian approaching briskly. His face filled with concern, he sinks respectfully to one knee in front of Abram.

"If you please," he says urgently, "the pharaoh would like to speak with you."

Abram's eyes are troubled as he grasps the servant firmly by his shoulders, raising him to his feet. "Of course," he answers.

The servant's face fills with relief, and the two men move swiftly toward the river. You follow a short way behind them, crossing the low stone bridge that spans the river.

After a short walk on the other bank, you see a huge brick enclosure—Abram and the servant disappear through the entrance. You break into a run, for you don't want to lose them—and hurtle through the entryway into a large, sunny court-yard. Across the court a pillared, two-story building stands, its lines simple and elegant. Abram strides confidently through an arched doorway—you follow only seconds later.

The cool, shadowy interior is a relief after the hot sun. Servants move busily up and down the stairs, stepping aside respectfully for Abram. Following closely behind, you reach the top of the stairs and find yourself in a huge meeting hall. Polished pillars gleam softly, separating the hall from a sheltered balcony. Chairs of burnished ebony line the walls, which are covered with brightly-painted murals. Your eyes are drawn instantly to the man on the dais, who is seated on a gilded throne. His kohl-lined eyes glitter beneath his tall headdress, and an ornate, jewel-studded collar falls half-way down his bare chest.

Abram approaches the pharaoh slowly; the two men's eyes lock, and hold.

Suddenly the pharaoh leaps to his feet, knocking the gilded throne into a dangerous rocking motion. "What is this you have done to me?" he cries in anguish. Descending from the dais in swift strides, he stretches an arm out toward Abram.

"Why did you not tell me that she was your wife?" The words are torn from the pharaoh, whose face is lined with grief and fear. "Why did you say, 'She is my sister,' so that I took her for my wife?"

The pharaoh claps his hands sharply, and several Egyptian women hurry into the hall — bringing with them an astonishingly beautiful woman.

Could this be Sarai? you think in awe — for this lady is more beautiful than anyone you have ever seen. You calculate swiftly that she must be at least sixty-five years old!

"Now then!" says the pharaoh sharply. "Here is your wife; take her and go!"

The room is suddenly full of Egyptian soldiers, their spears bristling. Abram's eyes soften as he looks at his wife; together they walk quickly out of the hall, surrounded by soldiers.

As you trot behind them, you wonder how the pharaoh knew that Sarai was Abram's wife. Surely she would not have suddenly decided to expose Abram's lie, for you remember that they had been here in Egypt for some time. Did God reveal the truth to the pharaoh? As you puzzle over the answer, you follow absently behind Abram and Sarai.

Suddenly the scene fades and you find yourself once again in the chariot.

"Now you will go forward in time," says the voice of the steed softly. "You may see a choice offered to Abram's nephew, Lot—or you may go farther forward in time, to see Hagar in the wilderness for the first time.

Hagar, you reflect. *She was Sarai's maid.* "Why was she in the wilderness?" you ask.

"Out of love for Abram, Sarai gave Hagar to her husband for a wife," replies the steed.

"Why would Sarai do that?" you wonder aloud.

"Sarai knew how desperately Abram wanted children," comes the answer. "She hoped that

Abram would have a child with Hagar. But Hagar taunted her mistress cruelly as soon as she knew that *she*—not Sarai—would bear Abram a child. Finally, Sarai could not stand Hagar's insolence any longer."

Lot's choice, or Hagar, you reflect. You take the reins thoughtfully in your hands, and make your decision.

If you decide to see Lot's choice, go to page 48.

If you decide to see Hagar in the wilderness for the first time, go to page 73.

(You Have Decided
to Be With Pharaoh in Egypt)

A roar of anger startles you as you find yourself in the midst of a swirl of activity. Egyptian slaves dressed in white linen bustle around you. You realize that you are somehow in the way—and a painful slap on the side of your head makes your ear ring.

"You! Don't just stand there—take this!" says the man who has boxed your ear. He shoves a huge platter piled high with bread into your hands and whirls to direct his attention elsewhere.

Dazed, you follow a young man carrying an enormous, brim-full jug, the top white with foam. He hurries across a moonlit courtyard, his eyes intent on the contents of his jug. You hurry behind him past several brick grain silos set against the side of an immense, two-story brick building. The full moon splashes the courtyard with soft light, and the sweet, gentle notes of a flute float from the second story above.

You follow hard on the heels of the servant as he darts into an arched entrance, then up a flight of stairs. You see the contents of his jug slosh over the rim and the pungent scent of beer assails your nostrils. Side-stepping the puddle, you bear your platter into an enormous hall. Amazed, you stand frozen in the doorway.

Tall stone pillars soar to the high ceiling and the walls are alive with brightly-painted murals. Chairs of polished, jet-black ebony line the walls, and low tables hold glittering oil lamps. On a dais at the opposite end of the room you see a gilded throne — *the man who is sitting there must be the pharaoh,* you decide. Men line one side of the hall, and women the opposite. Just now, all eyes are on dancing girls in the center of the vast room.

Weighted disks swing from the ends of long, dark braids as the girls bend far backward to the slow tune of the flutes and harp. Other musicians clap, accentuating the rhythm as the girls move like reeds on the river of music.

"Over there!" hisses a voice in your ear, as a sharp pinch on your arm reminds you that you are probably supposed to do something with your platter.

You hurry across the room to the women's side where you bow respectfully, offering the bread to the first lady. Her kohl-lined eyes glitter appreciatively as she surveys the variety of breads on the platter. Her heavy, jewelled collar and intricate gold armlet flash and sparkle in the light of the lamps. A glance at the other women reveals that all of them are adorned with gold and jewels, their hair is ornately curled, and sparkling headdresses encircle their foreheads.

After all the ladies have made their selection, you take your place along the wall with the other servants. You watch the pharaoh idly, until suddenly a woman — more beautiful than any woman you have ever seen — walks gracefully to his throne. Laughter and chatter cease at her entrance, and you feel an undercurrent of fear rippling through the hall.

"Who is she?" you whisper to the young servant

next to you. "Why does everyone seem afraid?"

"Sh!" he hisses, "That is Sarai. I have heard that it is because of her that our women are cursed."

"What?" you ask in confusion.

He puts a finger on his lips and motions you to follow him. No one sees you both slip quietly from the room and out onto the moonlit terrace. You follow the young man into the deep shadow of a pillar.

"Now," you begin, "did you say that is Sarai?"

"Yes—the sister of Abram, who lives on the other side of the river," he answers quietly. "Abram is a visitor here from Canaan, where there is a famine. Our pharaoh gave him permission to live here and graze his flocks. But there is something wrong," he adds, a puzzled frown creasing his brow, "for our women have been cursed from the day that Pharaoh took Sarai into his house."

You think carefully before you ask, "Who told Pharaoh that Sarai was Abram's sister?"

The young man's eyes widen in surprise. "Why, Abram did—Pharaoh wished to have her for one of his wives as soon as he learned of her exceeding beauty. She is not like any of his other wives!"

"But what do you mean," you question, "about your women being cursed?"

He shakes his head mournfully. "How can you not know that from the moment Sarai entered the royal house, not one woman has borne a child! How can the gods send a curse like that, unless. . ." his voice trails off.

"Unless," you continue softly, "Sarai is not supposed to belong to Pharaoh?"

"Exactly!" he exclaims, nodding vigorously. "I have heard," he says confidingly, "that Pharaoh has sent for Abram—*then* we shall find the answer to this puzzle! Come! We must return," the young man says, tugging you back into the hall.

Just as you get there, a servant rushes past you both to flatten himself before the throne of Pharaoh. You cannot hear what he says, for he is too far away, but a ripple of excitement spreads through the room.

All heads turn as a tall, bearded man strides confidently into the room. His multi-colored tunic sets him apart from the Egyptians, who are garbed in stark white. The man approaches Pharaoh as an equal, but his pleasant face is troubled. The pharaoh's kohl-lined eyes glitter beneath his tall headdress, and an ornate jewel-studded collar falls half-way down his bare chest.

A whispered "Abram" skitters through the room, and the music ceases. All eyes are on the two men.

Abram approaches the pharaoh and their eyes lock.

"What is this you have done to me?" cries the pharaoh in anguish. He leaps to his feet, knocking the carved throne into a dangerous sway. Descending from the dais in swift strides, he stretches an arm out toward Abram.

"Why did you not tell me that she was your wife?" The words are torn from the pharaoh, whose face is lined with grief and fear. "Why did you say, 'She is my sister,' so that I took her for my wife?"

Your gaze moves to Sarai, standing serene and beautiful at the foot of the dais. You calculate swiftly that she must be at least sixty-five years old, and are astonished—for she is obviously in the very prime of her life.

"Now then!" says the pharaoh sharply. "Here is your wife; take her and go!"

The room is suddenly full of Egyptian soldiers, their spears bristling. Abram's eyes soften as he looks at his wife; together they walk quickly out of the hall, surrounded by soldiers.

You decide to follow them, and stow your nearly-empty platter on a low table in the shadows. You wonder how Pharaoh knew that Sarai was Abram's wife—surely she would not have suddenly decided to expose Abram's lie, for you remember that they had been here in Egypt for some time. Did God reveal the truth to Pharaoh?

Suddenly the scene fades, as you find yourself once again in the chariot.

"Now you will go forward in time," says the voice of the steed softly. "You may see a choice offered to Abram's nephew, Lot—or you may go farther forward in time, to see Hagar in the wilderness for the first time."

Hagar, you reflect. *She was Sarai's maid.* "Why was she in the wilderness?" you ask.

"Out of love for Abram, Sarai gave Hagar to her husband for a wife," replies the steed.

"Why would Sarai do that?" you wonder aloud.

"Sarai knew how desperately Abram wanted children." comes the answer. "She hoped that Abram would have a child with Hagar. But Hagar taunted her mistress cruelly as soon as she knew that she, and not Sarai, would bear Abram a child. Finally, Sarai could not stand Hagar's insolence any longer."

Lot's choice, or Hagar, you reflect. You take the reins thoughtfully in your hands and make your decision.

**If you decide to see Lot's choice,
go to page 48.**

**If you decide to see Hagar
in the wilderness, go to page 73.**

(You Have Decided
to See Lot's Choice)

"Ouch!" You clap your hand to your aching nose; a trickle of blood runs into your mouth. You lift your forearm swiftly to block the next punch, for a stormy young face confronts you.

"Hey!" you shout in irritation. "Why are you punching me?"

"Are you one of Abram's herdsmen?" the boy asks suspiciously, his eyes hostile.

"So what if I am?" you ask, for you are growing angry.

He puts his fists up menacingly, scowling fiercely. "I asked you if you are one of Abram's herdsmen!"

You decide in a hurry that you are definitely on Abram's side, whatever the dispute. "Yes," you bellow, advancing purposefully toward the boy, "I am. What difference does that make?"

He backs a step or two away, frustrated malice glittering in his eyes. "You take your cattle someplace else to graze, do you hear?" his voice rises shrilly. "I'll get Lot's strongest herdsmen to teach you a lesson if you don't get out of here!"

Paying no attention to the sharp pain in your nose, you wish you could punch him out—but you decide regretfully that you should try to find out what you can about Lot instead of teaching this little coward a lesson.

A swift glance at the grassy slopes of the hills is enough to show you that you are in the midst of more livestock than you have ever seen together in one place in your life. Sheep, goats, and cattle graze contentedly for miles in every direction. Shading your eyes from the brilliant sun, you peer up the slopes at a large tent set apart from the others. Reflecting that the largest tent probably belongs to Abram, you turn your steps up the gentle incline.

"Ha! I knew you wouldn't fight!" taunts the boy when you are out of range of retaliation. Angry blood throbs in your ears, but you press your lips firmly together and walk on toward the tent. *With any luck,* you think wrathfully, *I may see him again!*

Hundreds of men are gathered around the tent shouting angrily. Into the furor steps Abram, and as he raises his hand for silence, the shouts subside into mutters.

Abram places his hands upon the shoulders of a younger man and says fondly, "Come, Lot, let us settle this matter." You look with interest at Lot—his face is sullen and spoiled. "Please let there be no strife between you and me, nor between my herdsmen and your herdsmen, for we are brothers."

Lot looks sulky, but Abram's face is filled with love and concern. The patriarch's voice is gentle as he continues, "Is not the whole land before you? Please separate from me; if you go to the left, then I will go to the right, or if you choose the right, then I will go to the left."

You edge a little closer, your eyes never leaving Lot's face. His lips curl in a sneer as he surveys the hills in every direction. You look down at the Jordan Valley below, which teems with life. As far as

you look in the valley, you see flowering trees and shrubs, and the sparkle of little brooks laughing through the fertile river plain. You turn in the opposite direction, where Abram's tent is on the summit of a hill. In that direction you see nothing that compares with the fertile Jordan River Valley.

At last Lot turns back to Abram. Smiling triumphantly, Lot stretches his hand toward the verdant valley below. "I shall choose the east," he says grandly.

What colossal nerve! you think angrily. *Abram graciously offered his nephew first choice, and he took the very best land!* Abram's herdsmen stand frozen in shocked silence; Lot's men grin gleefully at the outcome.

"Ho!" murmurs a shepherd at your elbow. "If we may go east, I shall go to Sodom!" His black eyes glitter with anticipation. "There is much amusement to be found in that fair city!"

You move away from this man, pondering the generosity of Abram, who not only shared his riches with his ungrateful nephew, but allowed him to take the choicest land. The sun is high overhead, and you sink wearily down in the shadow of an outcropping rock. You lie back and close your eyes, listening to the sleepy drone of bees.

You jump at a gentle touch on your shoulder. Confused, you realize that you must have fallen asleep. Abram's kind face smiles down at you.

"It grows cooler, my son — too cool to sleep without any kind of covering," he says.

You leap to your feet, disoriented. Abram's eyes are dreamy and faraway. "Look around you, my son," he says softly. "The Lord has told me that all the land I see He will give to me and my descendants forever—*forever!*" He shakes his head in wonder. "He has promised that He will make my descendants as numerous as the dust of the earth; so that if anyone can number the dust of the earth, then my descendants can also be numbered. Imagine!"

Abram's face shines with gratitude and reverence. He moves dreamily away, and you see the shimmering white chariot just ahead of you. Swiftly, you climb inside.

"Here is your choice," says the steed quietly. "You may see the covenant agreement between the Lord and his servant, Abram. Or you may go a little farther forward to see the battle of nine kings. Which will you choose?"

You think carefully, then make your decision.

If you decide to see the covenant, go to page 69.

If you decide to see the battle of nine kings, go to page 54.

(You Have Decided to See the Battle of Nine Kings)

You find yourself in the midst of chaos. The chariot has disappeared, and you are crouching against a huge boulder. An arrow hisses past your ear and a sword clangs against the rock inches from your head. Dazed, you shake your head to clear your senses, dropping even lower behind the boulder.

Your heart thuds as you peer cautiously from behind the stone. The flat grey landscape before you is filled with soldiers fighting for their lives and the bodies of those who have already lost the battle. Grim-faced men face each other with short sickle swords, and arrows slice through the air with a hiss of death. The acrid smell of blood mixed with the salty grey earth makes you nauseous. Suddenly, you jump in terror as a heavy axe embeds itself in the ground at your feet.

A huge hand grips your shoulder painfully. "So! Do you like the sight of battle?" asks a man's deep voice. The question makes you shudder. His eyes bore into your own, and his vise-like grip tightens. "Answer me! *Do you enjoy the sight of battle?'"* You shake your head miserably, wishing desperately for the chariot. You notice that the man's eyes are weary and discouraged.

A tired sigh escapes him, and he leans heavily against the rock. "I have seen too many battles," he says quietly, wiping the sweat from his brow with a massive forearm.

ily, as the sickening din of battle rages on behind you. His face is smeared with blood and dirt and is etched with deep lines of pain. "What are you doing here, youngster?" he asks quietly. "This is no place for you."

"Well," you stammer, "I didn't choose to come here." *That's for sure*! you think. You hesitate for a moment, and then ask, "Why are you fighting? Who are these armies?"

"When kings wish to fight," he answers bitterly, "their people do not have much choice." The man's tired eyes survey the battle wearily. "Nine kings wage war today—and it does not seem to me that it is going well for my king."

"Who is your king?" you ask curiously.

A rueful chuckle escapes the man's parched lips. "I wage war this day for the king of Sodom, youngster. But I am glad that I have already moved my wife out of that wicked city. I'll fight no more battles for the king of Sodom!"

A blood-chilling scream pierces the air only a yard or so away from you and the sickening sound of metal meeting bone makes your stomach churn. The man's eyes narrow, and he grasps you firmly.

"Listen to me," he hisses, as he glances warily over your shoulder. "You must get away while you can—and so must I! Make no sound, and follow me closely. We'll be making for that ridge over there. Come!"

The man breaks into a crouching run, making for the closest group of broken rocks. You glance swiftly over your shoulder and follow, your heart hammering. Beads of sweat sting your eyes as your feet slip queasily on the damp salt flats. A final lurch brings you to the rocks, where you sink back, panting.

"No time to rest!" the man's voice is desperately urgent. "Come!"

After what seems like hours of scuttling dangerously from rock to rock, the noise of battle is at last far behind you. You and your companion fling yourselves gratefully against a cool, flat rock. Your sides are heaving and your throat aches with thirst.

"We aren't safe yet, youngster—but we may rest for just a moment, I think."

A *moment*! you think in despair. "Surely we're safe now," you protest feebly. "The battle is way back there!"

The man's eyes widen in surprise. "We're in no danger from the battle youngster," he answers. "But the victorious soldiers will plunder Sodom— and we're perilously close to it!"

He stiffens suddenly, placing a finger urgently over his lips. The sound of faltering footsteps drawing nearer sends chills up your spine. The man grips his axe firmly, crouching low.

A boy about your age stumbles wearily into view. You breathe again, and your companion's grip on his battle axe slackens slightly.

"Oh!" gasps the boy as he sees the man. "Don't kill me!"

The man grins tiredly. "Do I look like I kill youngsters?"

The boy leans exhaustedly against the rock. "I must reach Abram the Hebrew quickly!" he quavers. "His nephew Lot has been taken captive!"

Electrified, you stiffen to attention. The man whistles low.

"Lot has been taken?" he asks, his brows lifting in surprise. "This *will* be interesting! Come — our paths lie together," the man says briskly. "Abram is living near Hebron, and my home is now there. We must make haste," he says firmly.

He beckons you swiftly and turns north; the boy springs to his side. Suddenly their retreating forms disappear from sight — the magnificent chariot of fire stands squarely in front of you.

Still awed by the flames that do not consume, you step slowly inside the chariot. The milky steed stands quietly, and the low, musical voice speaks again.

"You have arrived at another choice," the voice says quietly. "You may go forward in time to see *Abraham* plead with the Lord to save Sodom, or you may stay here to see *Abram* rescue Lot. Which shall you choose?"

You remember that your quest is to learn why Abram's name was changed—and you feel sure that you could not learn the answer by going forward to a time when his name was already changed. You find yourself eager to see Abram again—and it would definitely be interesting to see him rescue Lot. But maybe you *should* choose to see him plead with the Lord. Thoughtfully, you take the reins in your hands and make your choice.

If you decide to see
Abram rescue Lot, go to page 60.

If you decide to see
Abraham plead with the Lord, go to page 85.

(You Have Decided
to See Abram Rescue Lot)

Blinking, you find yourself in velvet-black night. The thin sliver of a crescent moon hangs suspended in a starry sky. Your back rests against a stone, and you hear the soft song of a brook rushing over boulders just beside you. Disoriented, you strain to see into the darkness.

At last your eyes become accustomed to the night. You see that you are on the slope of a low hill overlooking a stream-fed plain. The glow of a huge circle of camp fires and torches reveals dozens of tents on the plain, and you wonder who is camping there. A sudden, bloodcurdling scream shatters the hushed night, and torches wink into life everywhere. Soon, torches light up the area, and you watch in fascination as the men stumble into each other in confusion.

Suddenly, the night grows even brighter as torch-bearing soldiers appear on the crest of the hills surrounding the camp. Battle cries echo from hill to hill as the soldiers pour down toward the encampment. It looks from here as if thousands of men are attacking the camp. Now screams of terror and shouts of confusion make your blood run cold. You glance nervously around, wondering if you are in any danger here—when suddenly you hear a deep voice roar above the sounds of battle below.

"Lot! Where are you?"

You scramble to your feet, for you are certain that the voice must belong to Abram. Cautiously, you make your way down the gentle slope of the hill, dashing from the cover of one rock to another. In the darkness, you hear the labored breathing of a man running toward you and before you can think, he plows heavily into you, knocking you flat on your back. Your heart leaps into your throat as he utters a curse and raises a bloody axe high above his head.

"Wait!" you scream in terror.

Cursing again, the man lowers the axe. "Out of my way, boy," he mutters.

You jump gratefully to your feet, your heart pounding. "Thank you!" you gasp as the man turns to go. "Wait!" you call out, and then seeing the look on his face, you stammer, "I mean, if you please, could you tell me who is camping down there and who is attacking?"

"We who were camped for the night are all who remain of the armies of Elam, Goiim, Shinar, and Ellasar," he answers wrathfully. "Abram— cursed be he—has pursued us since we defeated the kings of Sodom and Gomorrah. I knew in my bones that there would be trouble over taking prisoners. Abram and his men have chased us for

miles — and we can run no further. I'll not risk
death another night! Abram can have his cursed
nephew, and his relatives, and his goods!"

The man stumbles up the hill, disappearing
from sight into the blackness. You see others running away, melting into the shadows of the low
hills. The sounds of battle have ceased now, and

you slowly approach the nearly-abandoned camp. A tall man, his shoulders broad and strong, strides toward the center.

"Lot!" he calls. "Where are you?"

"Uncle! I am here!" cries a younger man racing into view. "I knew you would rescue us!"

"Praise be to God Most High!" exclaims Abram. The two men embrace amid the cheers of Abram's men.

You notice in surprise that the sky is lighter—a rosy glow over the low hills to the east announces the dawn.

"Come!" says Abram. "Gather your people and your goods together. It is time to start for home!"

The men spring into action and amidst the bustle you look at Abram carefully. *His face is a good face,* you think to yourself—*honest, and God-fearing. Lot looks nice, too—but he does not have the strength in his eyes that I see in his uncle's.*

A swirling, bright-white mist obscures your view, and you find yourself once again in the chariot of fire. The extraordinary steed stands patiently—but something is puzzling you.

"There is something you do not understand, my friend?" says the steed softly.

"Well," you say, "I thought that Abram was about eighty years old when he rescued Lot. He certainly didn't *look* like an old man."

A soft, bell-like tinkle chimes musically—

startled, you realize that the steed must be laughing.

"Oh, little one—he is eighty years old, but he is not an old man!"

"Not old?" you question.

"No, of course not," the steed answers. "You must realize that Abram's time is only about four hundred years after the flood. That is not very long—and before the flood, living at least nine hundred years was common. So you see that a man of eighty is not old."

Satisfied, you take the reins in your hands; you are eager to see what will come next.

"Your choice now," says the steed quietly, "is between two times in Abram's future. You may see his meeting with Melchizedek outside Salem, on his way home with Lot, or you may go farther forward in the future to see the birth of Ishmael, his son by Hagar. Which shall it be?"

You wonder briefly which would be more helpful in your quest, and decide that you have no idea. Swiftly, you make your decision as you pull the reins taut.

If you decide to see the birth of Ishmael, go to page 78.

If you decide to see Abram meet Melchizedek, go to page 65.

(You Have Decided to See Abram Meet Melchizedek)

You find yourself deposited gently on a steep, grassy slope. A deep valley separates you from the wooded hills on the other side, where the brick walls of a fortified city crown the summit. Early-morning sunshine splashes down the green slopes, and birds trill joyously from every tree. A sudden rough nudge against the back of your knees startles you into whirling around — and you discover that you are standing in the path of a herd of goats. Playfully, the little goat nearest you tugs on your tunic — soon you are completely surrounded.

To your surprise, you see that the hill behind you is covered with cattle, sheep, and goats — more than you have ever seen together at one time in your life. You scratch absently the rough-coated goat at your knees until you realize that he is actually trying to eat your tunic! Carefully, you pull the soggy cloth from his mouth and push your way through the herd, heading for the valley below.

When you reach the valley floor you see that hundreds of people are making their way slowly south, leading donkeys laden with goods. Happy laughter and bursts of song fill the air, and you recognize the figures of Abram and Lot at the head of the throng.

A woman in the crowd suddenly notices and points to a solitary figure making his way carefully down the hill. A hush begins to spread through the happy crowd as all eyes turn to the man on the hill making his way towards them.

He is clothed in a snowy-white tunic and sunlight flashes from a simple golden circlet on his head. As he reaches the valley, the crowd parts for him and he approaches Abram, whose face is solemn. You press forward, eager to see what will happen next.

"Who is that?" you whisper to a girl standing next to you.

Her astonished eyes turn toward you. "That is Melchizedek, king of Salem. He is priest of El Elyon, the most high God."

"King of Salem?" you puzzle, frowning. You had thought that the city on the hill was Jerusalem. Maybe, you reflect, Salem was the name *before* the city came to be called Jerusalem; you resolve to ask your steed for the answer.

"Oh! Isn't it amazing that the king should come to Abram like this?" sighs the girl. "He must be a mighty man of God!"

"Abram?!" you question in mild defense. "I should say he is! But why is Melchizedek so special?"

Again, the girl stares at you in astonishment. "I thought everyone knew," she answers. "Melchizedek is without father or mother—he has no beginning and no ending. He is made like the Son of God!"

Your thoughts in a jumble, you wrest your attention back to Abram, who is solemnly bowing before the king. The crowd is silent as the rich voice of Melchizedek proclaims, "Blessed be Abram of El Elyon, Creator of heaven and earth; and blessed be El Elyon, who has delivered your enemies into your hand."

You can see from here that the king is offering bread and wine to Abram—and you reflect in wonder upon another King, whose father was God, and who also offered bread and wine. *How could any human king have no father or mother?* you wonder. The scene fades from view as you find yourself back in the chariot of fire.

"You have questions, little one?" the steed's voice is gentle.

"Yes, I do—lots of them!" you answer. "First of all—is Salem the same place as Jerusalem?"

"Yes, they are one and the same," comes the answer.

"Well, then, who is Melchizedek? A girl told me that he had no father or mother, and that he was made like the Son of God! Is Melchizedek . . . can he be Jesus?"

The steed does not answer for a moment, and your heart hammers in the silence. At last, the voice begins softly, "You are asking if you have seen what your modern theologians would call a pre-Bethlehem appearance of Jesus. Hebrew tradition holds that Melchizedek was Shem—who is still alive at this time. Others would tell you that Melchizedek was simply a king, around whom myths grew to increase his importance."

"But," you stammer, "who do *you* say he is?"

"Have patience, little one," says the voice gently. "Now you see in a mirror dimly, but there will be a day when you shall know fully—just as you are fully known."

You have a strong feeling that you are going to have to be satisfied with this answer—and also that your heart knows what the truth is.

The quiet voice sparkles in the silence, "Now I shall take you to see the covenant between the Lord and Abram.

Your heart hammering in excitement, you pick up the reins.

Go to page 69.

(The Covenant)

You find yourself in a familiar grove of oak trees; not far away you see Abram stooping over, busy with something on the ground. Hesitantly, you approach him—and disgust washes over you as you see what he is doing. He straightens and turns to you, a welcoming smile on his face. You look in revulsion at the dead carcasses of animals on the ground at his feet.

"What troubles you, my friend?" Abram asks gently, his smile fading.

"Are those sacrifices?" you ask, pointing at the lifeless heifer, goat, ram, and two birds.

"Yes," Abram says slowly, watching your face carefully. "My Lord has instructed me to bring them—why are you so disgusted?"

You struggle with yourself, for you have never understood why God would ask for the sacrifice of innocent animals. At last you blurt, "I don't understand. How does a sacrifice honor God?"

"Ours is not always to understand, my son, but to obey," answers Abram gently. "A sacrifice covers the sin of mankind—for when our father Adam fell, was it not necessary that an animal die to provide a covering for his shame?"

A sudden realization bursts upon you like lightning—*a sacrifice to cover sin! Was it possible that God instructed men to sacrifice animals to point to the One who would be the perfect sacrifice for the sins of all?* Abram has watched your changing expression and now adds softly, "The death of the animals is swift and painless, my young friend. But I think that you understand better now."

You nod in agreement. "Please," you ask humbly, "do you know why God asked you to bring these animals today?"

"I am to arrange the animals for a covenant agreement," he answers. "Look—they are arranged in that manner."

You stare uncomprehending at the animals—cut in two and laid each half opposite the other, with the exception of the birds, which are not cut.

"In a solemn covenant between two parties," Abram continues gently, "the agreeing partners join hands and walk between the halves of slain animals. This means that the partners are pledging that the agreement will be kept even in the midst of blood and death."

The slanting rays of the setting sun cast long fingers of shadow over the sacrifices; Abram fades from sight as the shimmering flames of the chariot enfold you.

"This is no longer a place for you, little one," says the steed quietly. "For the Lord himself will soon come."

"Will God and Abram then walk between the

animals?" you question eagerly.

"No, child," the voice answers softly. "Abram will be cast into a deep sleep—and the Lord shall pass alone through the sacrifices."

You frown in concentration. "But I thought that in a covenant, the two agreeing parties walked together," you say haltingly.

"Normally, that is true," says the steed. "In this case, however, it is the Lord who initiates the agreement—it is a promise given to Abram without any strings attached. Today the Lord will also give Abram the prophecy regarding his descendants' captivity in Egypt."

"What prophecy?" you question, startled.

Faint musical chimes, like the tinkling of crystal bells, quiver in the silence of the iridescent flames. "Read the Word, little one, and you will learn that the Lord told Abram that his descendants would be strangers in a land that is not theirs for four hundred years. For at least part of that time, they would be enslaved and oppressed. The Lord said that He would then judge the nation that they serve, and afterward they would come out with many possessions— the fourth generation in the strange land shall return to the promised land."

Awed, you whisper, "Does that mean Egypt? And *did* the fourth generation return here?"

"Remember," chimes the voice, "that Joseph—

Abram's great-grandson—was sold into slavery in Egypt. Joseph was the first generation. Levi, one of Joseph's older brothers, had a son named Kohath. Kohath was the second generation, and had a son, Amram—the third generation. Aram's son, the fourth generation in Egypt, was Moses."

Your head in a daze, you resolve to search the Scriptures yourself when you return to your time. Absentmindedly, you take the smooth leather reins into your hands.

"Now I shall take you forward to the time," says the voice, "when the Lord warns Abraham that He is going to destroy Sodom—and Abraham pleads with Him to spare the city."

You wonder why Abraham would care whether or not Sodom is destroyed—until you remember Lot. *Abraham is still looking out for his nephew!* you reflect in amazement.

Go to page 85.

(You Have Decided to See Hagar in the Wilderness)

The chariot deposits you on burning sand and disappears as suddenly as it appeared. A fierce wind whips your tunic and grains of sand lash your bare skin. The sun glares down mercilessly, scorching the barren dunes. Shimmering heat waves make the entire desolate landscape look like an eerie, shifting kaleidoscope seen in a nightmare. Your eyes burn from heat and the stinging sand; you shield them with your forearm and peer anxiously around you.

Through eyelids nearly shut against the burning wind, you think you catch a glimpse of green over the largest dune. Stumbling forward into the blast, you climb to the top of a dune. Looking down from the summit, you see several thorny trees below, their bent trunks testimony to the ferocity of the wind. You scramble down, half slipping and half running, to land in a heap at the base of the dune.

Several trees cluster around a rough well built of stones. The wind is a bit less fierce in this hollow, and as your ears grow accustomed to the relative silence, you are surprised to hear a woman sobbing quietly. You turn to the direction of her cries.

She is young, and she is crumpled over in grief against the rough stone well. You know that this must be Hagar, Sarai's slave—and you know that she must be carrying Abram's child in her body. You remember that Hagar treated her mistress with contempt when she learned that she—not Sarai—would bear Abram's child, and that, as a result, Sarai angrily sent her away. *Well,* you think, *Sarai was wrong to be so cruel—but Hagar was wrong too, for treating Sarai hatefully just because she couldn't have children. It is always wrong to gloat over someone else's problem!*

Suddenly, the roar of the wind overhead dies away completely and is replaced with a silence so complete that you find yourself wishing for some noise again. Hagar has noticed too—you see her lift her tear-stained face, her eyes wide in wonder. She pulls herself to her knees by the well, gazing in awe at something that has suddenly appeared in front of her.

"Hagar," says a voice so beautiful you feel as if your heart must melt, "Sarai's maid, where have you come from and where are you going?"

"I am fleeing from the presence of my mistress, Sarai," the girl quavers.

"Return to your mistress," says the voice, "and submit yourself to her authority."

You cannot see the speaker from your position, but you can see that the whole area is bathed with

radiance so bright and so beautiful that the white-hot desert sun seems dirty and pale by comparison. The presence of power is almost too intense to bear — and yet you wish it would never leave. Shaken, you realize that the angel — for so the presence of power must be — is speaking once again.

"Behold, you are with child, and you shall bear a son, and you shall call his name Ishmael, because the Lord has heard of your misery. And he will be a wild donkey of a man; his hand will be against everyone and everyone's hand will be against him, and he will live in hostility toward all his brothers."

The radiance fades, and the deep silence is shattered by the return of the howling wind. Trembling violently, you pull yourself to your feet. Hagar's amazed eyes meet yours, and you wonder if your face is as awestricken as hers. She turns her face toward Heaven and lifts her arms in adoration. "Thou art a God who sees!" she cries, her face uplifted and filled with love. Turning back to you, her eyes grow puzzled. "Have I even remained alive here after seeing Him?"

You find that you cannot speak, but she does not seem to care. Her face is still filled with awe as she turns her faltering steps away from you.

Hagar and the landscape fade from view as you find yourself once more in the leaping white flames of the chariot. The steed's voice carries quietly in the stillness. "Remember, child, the promise given to Hagar this day. The sons and daughters of Ishmael will always trouble the world.

"Now for your decision. Would you like to see the birth of Hagar's son, Ishmael? Or would you like to see Hagar in the wilderness for the second time, after Sarah has driven her away forever?"

Wondering which choice would be best, you take the cool reins in your hands. Thinking carefully, you make your decision and pull the reins taut.

**If you decide to see
the birth of Ishmael, go to page 78.**

**If you decide to see Hagar in the
wilderness the second time, go to page 111.**

(You Have Decided to Go to the Birth of Ishmael)

Gentle breezes rustle leaves above your head as you find yourself beneath a gnarled oak tree. Low mountains rise to the west, and the land slopes down gradually toward the east, where you catch a glimpse of water on the horizon. Tents line the grassy incline and the hills teem with livestock. From the largest tent, a lusty newborn wail can be heard.

A voice close at hand startles you, and you see two men sitting on a large boulder a few feet away from you. "Well!" chuckles one. "So Abram has an heir at last!"

The other grins. "Won't Sarai be pleased!" he snickers. "Her slave has presented Abram with the child Sarai could never give him!"

"Abram—'exaulted father'!" guffaws the first. "He finally has ONE child!"

Both men double up with laughter at this, wiping eyes streaming with tears of mirth. Gulping for air, the first man speaks again.

"I'm just surprised that the old fool took Hagar for a concubine at all!" he sneers. "If Abram is crazy enough to believe that God will make his descendants as numerous as the dust of the earth. . ." he pauses, his shoulders shaking, "then why didn't he

trust God to bring forth his 'nation' out of Sarai's barren womb?"

Startled, you realize that you never thought of that before. Now you remember that God *had* made that promise *long* before Sarai gave Hagar to Abram—at least ten years, according to the Bible. Did Abram give up on God's promise, and take matters into his own hands? You resolve to find out what you can about this when you return to your own time, and then you turn your attention back to the men.

"So, what will Abram call this heir—have you heard?"

"He is to be called Ishmael— 'God hears,'" the other answers. "Hagar insists that God himself has named the child, so 'Ishmael' it will be."

Their voices fade as the landscape is blotted from view by the flames of the chariot. The low, musical voice of the steed is soothing.

"Now your choice lies between the past and the future. You may go back in time to see the covenant between the Lord and Abram, or forward to see Hagar in the wilderness for the second time."

"But . . ." you stammer, "will either of those choices help me on my quest?"

"Little one, you should understand that everything you can learn about God's people will help you all your life long," comes the gentle answer.

"You mean," you say meditatively, "that even things that happened almost four thousand years ago are like pointers to the truth?"

"Exactly!" chimes the voice joyfully. "You are understanding very well!"

Flushed with pleasure at the compliment, you pick up the smooth leather reins.

**If you decide to see
the covenant, go to page 69.**

**If you decide to see
Hagar in the wilderness again, go to page 111.**

(You Have Decided to Learn About Abram's Name Change)

A pale sliver of moon hangs high in the velvet black sky and a cool night breeze whispers among leaves overhead. You are straining to see in the darkness when suddenly your wrist is gripped in a vise-like grasp.

"What are you doing here?" growls a voice menacingly. "Did you think to steal some of my sheep?"

"No, no," you protest nervously, as you look into the eyes of your captor. "I couldn't sleep," you continue, thinking quickly, "and I just wanted to walk a little."

The grip relaxes. "Very well," the young man sighs. "Already this night I have fought off the hyenas — listen! They are out there still."

Eerie, sobbing laughs float through the still night — your skin prickles at the sound. The young man turns abruptly, his eyes staring intently into the darkness. Your eyes, accustomed now to the night, pick out the forms of sheep sleeping contentedly in a huge flock.

"The hyenas are far away," he says at last, satisfied. "Come. Share my meal — I am glad of your company." He rummages in a skin bag, drawing out a large packet. Sinking down to the ground, he breaks a flattened loaf into two pieces, holding one out to you with a smile.

You sit beside him on the ground, settling your back comfortably against a boulder. Stars blaze through the swaying leaves overhead, and you

munch contentedly. "Thank you—this is good!" you say honestly.

The shepherd grins. "My mother's bread is always delicious," he answers, "and she always gives me enough for ten shepherds! Sometimes even Abraham shares bread with me," he adds proudly.

Eagerly, you ask, "Do you know why Abram's name was changed to Abraham?"

The young man's eyes narrow, and he regards you with suspicion. "Are you laughing at him?" he asks, his voice rising in anger.

"No—of course not!" you respond. "Who would laugh at him?"

The scowl fades from his face and he sighs. "A lot of people are laughing," he says quietly. "They find it amusing that a man with one son, Ishmael, would change his name from Abram— exalted father—to Abraham, father of a multitude. But *I* think," the young man says defiantly, "that if the Lord says Abraham will have a son by Sarah—that's what will happen!"

"But what about Ishmael?" you ask, frowning. "Will he be left out?"

"Of course not!" answers the shepherd. "The Lord has promised Abraham that He will bless Ishmael—that he will become the father of twelve princes, and will become a great nation. That's hardly being left out!"

"I still don't see why it was necessary to change Abram's name," you puzzle aloud.

"That's easy!" the shepherd responds, laughing delightedly. "Because the Lord established a new covenant with Abraham. Before, the Lord God gave Abram the land. Now He has said that He will make Abraham the father of a multitude of *nations!* Is that not marvelous?"

The shepherd suddenly springs to his feet, staring intently into the night. "Something is wrong—I must go!" he calls over his shoulder urgently.

He bounds out of sight over a low rise, and the chariot stands before you. You climb thoughtfully aboard, still wondering *how* the change of Abraham's name could possibly have anything to do with us today.

"Your choice now is between two times," the quiet voice says. "You may see the birth of Abraham's grandsons, Jacob and Esau, more than sixty years in the future, or you may travel even farther in time to see Jacob's name changed. Which will you choose?"

Still puzzling, you make your decision.

If you decide to see the birth of Jacob and Esau go to page 133.

If you decide to see Jacob's name change, go to page 136.

(You Have Decided to See Abraham Plead With the Lord)

You find yourself on the grassy slope of a ridge of mountains, beneath the shade of a cluster of gnarled, old, oak trees. Shafts of sunlight pierce the leafy canopy above your head and the leaves toss gently in the warm breeze. Just beneath the crown of the hill you see the largest of many tents in the area and as you are watching, four robed figures appear framed in the tent door. You watch intently as they approach the oak grove, and you flatten yourself against the cool bark of a tree.

Two of the men—their faces noble and stern—stride off down the slope, their eyes seemingly intent on a place far distant in the valley below. Abraham and the remaining man halt suddenly within the grove of trees. You cannot see the stranger's face, for the folds of his headdress conceal it.

The stranger speaks, and the quality of his voice sends chills racing down your spine—it is unlike any voice you have ever heard before and yet, instead of being frightened, you are somehow drawn to the voice that says, "The outcry of Sodom and Gomorrah is indeed great, and their sin is exceedingly grave. I will go down now, and see if they have done entirely according to the outcry which has come to me; and if not, I will know."

You can see the color drain from Abraham's face as he says quietly, "Suppose there are fifty righteous within the city; wilt Thou indeed sweep it

away and not spare the place for the sake of the fifty righteous who are in it?" His voice grows stronger as he continues. "Far be it from Thee to do such a thing, to slay the righteous with the wicked, so that the righteous and the wicked are treated alike. Far be it from Thee! Shall not the judge of all the earth deal justly?"

You catch your breath in the silence that follows, waiting for the answer of the Lord.

The deep voice responds quietly, "If I find in

Sodom fifty righteous people, then I will spare the whole place on their account."

Abraham shifts nervously as he speaks again. "Now behold, I have ventured to speak to the Lord, although I am but dust and ashes." His voice trembles slightly as he continues, "Suppose the fifty righteous are lacking five, wilt Thou destroy the whole city because of five?"

The hairs on the back of your neck prickle uncomfortably as you listen to Abraham. Silence floods the hillside; it feels as if nature itself is holding its breath.

"I will not destroy it if I find forty-five there."

"Suppose forty are found there?" Abraham questions.

"I will not do it on account of the forty."

Fear and determination struggle visibly on Abraham's honest countenance. "Oh may the Lord not be angry, and I shall speak; suppose thirty are found there?"

Patiently, the deep voice answers, "I will not destroy the city if I find thirty there."

"Now behold," quavers Abraham, his face ashen, "I have ventured to speak to the Lord; suppose twenty are found there?"

"I will not destroy it on account of the twenty."

Abraham falls to his knees, tears coursing down his face.

"Oh may the Lord not be angry," Abraham pleads, "And I shall speak only this once more; what if only ten are found there?"

In the complete silence that follows, you notice that there is not a whisper of a breeze nor a single trill of a bird. You press yourself miserably against the tree trunk, wondering at the patience of the Lord—and the audacity of Abraham! Unseen hosts wait for the Lord's answer, as the earth wheels through His universe.

Infinitely loving and endlessly patient the voice answers, "I will not destroy the city if I find ten righteous there."

Nature erupts into life again; the leaves whisper, birds call, streams laugh, and you can breathe again. Through swimming eyes you notice your chariot waiting quietly in the grove. You scramble aboard, awed at what you have just seen.

The musical voice of the milky steed chimes softly, "Your choice now is this: you may see the angels warn Lot of Sodom's doom, or you may go to see Lot's sons-in-law in Sodom."

Lot's sons-in-law? you wonder. *Why weren't they with their father-in-law?* Hastily you decide.

If you decide to see the angels warn Lot, go to page 89.

If you decide to stay with the sons-in-law, go to page 100.

(You Have Decided to See the Angels Warn Lot)

You find yourself standing before the gates of a vast, walled city. Twilight is stealing over the plain, and the air of the approaching evening is chilly. Robed merchants busily stow their goods in wagons, preparing to leave this place of commerce. You notice one man in particular—he is casting worried glances over his shoulder as he flings the last of his flasks carelessly into a huge basket on the back of his donkey.

You approach him and ask, "Excuse me, please—is this the city of Sodom?"

He shudders violently. "Oh yes, my friend— and if you're wise, you'll get away from here before night falls! I have been delayed today— usually I am safely in my home away from this city long before now!"

You squint anxiously into the gathering gloom where shadowy figures hurry away from the city. One lone man sits in the blackness, just outside the gates. Hesitantly, you glance toward him.

"You'd better listen to me!" warns the merchant again. "This evil city is no place for a youngster!" He gives his donkey a sharp slap, and they move away in the dark.

A sudden wind rises, moaning eerily. You move

toward the one person left by the city gates. His eyes gleam white in the darkness. Suddenly, he leaps to his feet—a startled exclamation torn from his throat. He stares into the night, then flings himself facedown upon the ground. Startled at his behavior, you flatten yourself against the wall of the city, still warm from the day's sun.

Two tall figures approach, heavily robed. They stop directly in front of the prostrate figure, and one of them raises him gently to his feet.

"Now behold, my lords," says the man who was on the ground in a voice tight with anxiety, "please turn aside into your servant's house. You may wash your feet and spend the night, and then go on your way early in the morning."

"No," answers a deep, rich voice. "We shall spend the night in the square."

Lot—for so he must be—moves in agitation. He whispers urgently to the two robed strangers and you cannot catch his words. He tugs on their arms, pulling them through the city gates. You have no choice but to follow, for the night is growing dark and you are *not* willing to stay here alone!

A blood-chilling scream suddenly shatters the stillness, followed by drunken laughter. Your throat goes dry and you quicken your pace to keep the three figures ahead of you in sight. Flames of torches set against brick houses leap wildly, flinging monstrous shadows down the black street.

A rectangle of light spills onto the street as the three figures open the door of a house. You break into a run, for you cannot escape the feeling that you dare not remain in the city alone.

You crash painfully into a huge man who looms out of the darkness. Terror crawls up your spine as he grips your arm tight.

"Oooooh," he croons awfully, "what a delicious youngster I've caught here. Come, let me show you what delights I can give you," he whispers close to your ear. His hands slide down your back, filling you with such intense disgust that your scream freezes in your throat.

In despair, you watch the open door begin to close behind Lot and his two companions. Desperate, you sink your teeth into your captor's forearm. Howling an oath, he breaks his grip just long enough to allow you to dash madly for the doorway. Frantically, you claw at the door, heedless of your bloodied fingers wedged in the tiny opening. At last, you are inside the courtyard. Lot bars the door behind you, and you cast yourself down in the corner, trembling so violently you could not possibly stand.

Lot and the two strangers disappear up a short stone stairway. The pounding of your heart slowly subsides as you watch three women move

calmly about, preparing a meal at the stone oven in the corner of the courtyard. The youngest of the women smiles at you, bringing you a cup brimming full with water from the well. You drink gratefully; you had not realized how thirsty you are.

Lot and the men return — *they look like ordinary men,* you think wonderingly, knowing that they are angels. Lot beckons you with a smile to join the group for dinner, and conversation ceases as the tasty meal is consumed.

A strange sound outside the house has been growing all through the meal, and finally you realize with a shudder that it is the sound of a huge number of angry people. Now a man bangs his fist on the door and yells, "Lot! Master of this house, come and open this door!" Lot's face is uneasy as he moves across the courtyard to the door and slides the wooden plank away to open it a tiny crack.

"Where are the men who came to you tonight?" a harsh voice cries from the doorway. "Bring them out to us that we may have relations with them." Drunken laughter and screams of delight make the hairs on the back of your neck rise. You glance quickly at the angels, who are rising to their feet.

Lot inches out into the street, closing the door firmly behind him. His voice rises as he pleads,

"Please, my brothers, do not act wickedly. Now behold, I have two daughters who are pledged to be married, but have not had relations with any man; please let me bring them out to you, and do to them whatever you like; only do nothing to these men, inasmuch as they have come under the shelter of my roof."

Horrified, you look at the youngest of Lot's daughters. Her face is white with fear, and you cannot believe that her own father would offer her to the wicked crowd outside. "How can he do that?" you whisper in anguish.

A fleeting ghost of a smile passes across her white lips. "It would be my duty, if I must," she whispers. "The safety and well-being of any guest in our home must come before our own."

"Stand aside," the harsh voice outside commands. "You came in as an alien," he says to Lot, "and already you are acting like a judge; now we will treat you worse than them!" You hear the wood of the door creak in protest as the throng in the street presses urgently against it. The sound of splintering wood strikes terror in your heart —where can you hide? The angels, however, seem calm. Crossing the courtyard swiftly, they open the door, pull Lot inside, and shut the door in one fluid motion.

Within the passing of one heartbeat, screams of terror and wails of anguish erupt from outside, and Lot looks questioningly at his guests. "They have been struck with blindness," one explains shortly. "Now let them try to find your door!"

The other angel speaks. "Whom else have you here? Sons-in-law, sons or daughters, and anyone else in the city who belongs to you, bring them out," he says, his face stern and unyielding. "For we are about to destroy this place. The sin of this city has become so great that the Lord has sent us to destroy this place and everyone in it."

A shimmering white radiance issues from one of the rooms facing the courtyard. You cross swiftly to the room, grateful to see the chariot of fire. Relieved, you climb quickly inside. "Why is Lot in this terrible city?" you ask in disgust.

The steed's voice is solemn as it answers, "Only God knows, little one. Lot has always known of its wickedness—even years ago when his uncle Abram gave him his choice of land and he chose the land near Sodom. It is not wise for a child of the Lord to place himself within temptation's iron grip. But now, I shall take you to morning," says the steed quietly, "where you shall see for yourself how the Lord hates the wickedness of this vile city."

Go to page 96.

(The Destruction of Sodom)

A fiery sun paints the plains bloodred in the chill dawn air. Jagged teeth of rocky hills bite into the sky to the west; to the east you see a walled city. With some dread, you turn your steps toward the city. Suddenly, six figures burst through the city gates, two of them leading and urging the rest of the group to hurry. As you jog toward them, you recognize Lot, his two daughters, his wife, and the angelic visitors. *So!* you think, *There were only four righteous people in Sodom after all! Abraham's pleading could not save the city!*

You hear one of the angels speak. "Flee for your lives! Do not look behind you, and do not stop anywhere in the valley; escape to the mountains, lest you be swept away!"

Lot's face pales as he exclaims, "Oh no, my lords! I cannot escape to the mountains, they are too far way! This disaster will overtake me and I will die!" His voice rises as he begs, "There is a town near enough to run to, and it is small. Please, let me go there so that my life may be saved." He gestures wildly into the distance.

The response is stern. "Very well, I will grant you this request also, not to overthrow the town of which you have spoken. But hurry there, for I cannot do anything until you reach it."

Lot and his wife and two daughters spring into a run and you race behind them, your heart pounding. The rising sun casts long, eerie shadows of your running figures; the shapes slither wildly over the grassy plains.

Your shadows shorten as the sun climbs higher over the horizon; your throat aches with thirst, and your lips are cracked and bleeding. Just when you feel you cannot run another inch, a small town appears at the foot of a hill.

The earth begins to tremble beneath you and you hear Lot shriek, "Don't look behind you! Hurry!" The figures of Lot and his daughters are growing smaller, but his wife has stopped and turned toward you, shading her eyes to gaze past you toward Sodom. The trembling of the earth swells until you feel like you are riding a wave in the sea. A blast of wind assaults you, hurtling dust and twigs against you in a stinging attack. The sun glows dimly red in the gathering darkness, partly blotted from sight by the debris whirling in the wind.

Finally, earth and sky erupt in a mighty roar— you press your hands tightly against your ears and squeeze your eyes shut against the blast. Your head is reeling as you flatten yourself against the heaving earth—you have never been so frightened in all your life and you realize with awe that you are in the midst of a judgement directly from the hand of the Lord.

After what seems like an eternity, the din ceases. Your ears still ringing, you open your eyes slowly—remembering NOT to look back toward Sodom. In the spot where you last saw Lot's wife, you now see—a violent shudder shakes you from head to foot. For there, rising from the barren plain, stands a twisted, chalky pillar of salt. The wind-whipped sand has already begun to erode the features, but you recognize the shape as that of Lot's wife. She has paid the penalty of disobeying the messengers of God.

The flames of the chariot blot the awful pillar from sight; gratefully, you step into in the quiet chariot behind the steed.

"It is time now for a decision," says the steed, and his soft voice is a balm for your still-aching ears. "I am permitted to take you back a little in time, to learn about Abram's name change—or forward to the birth of Abraham's son, Isaac."

Aha! you think gleefully—remembering your quest. *This decision will not be hard to make*—or should you take the less obvious choice? Thinking carefully, you decide.

If you decide to learn about Abram's name change, go to page 81.

If you decide to see Isaac's birth, go to page 103.

(You Have Decided to Stay With Lot's Sons-in-law)

The wind-tossed flames of a torch make shadows jump eerily in the inky darkness. Wild, drunken laughter makes your skin crawl as you peer anxiously down a near-deserted street. You see two men locked in a passionate embrace, swaying crazily in the shadows not far from you—and disgust floods through your veins. Light spills out from an open door just behind you, and you edge cautiously inside.

The stench of stale beer mingles with filth, and you see several men sprawled in low chairs. Their faces are wrathful and belligerent, and you can see at a glance that they are very drunk.

"What was your crazy old father-in-law yammering about, anyway?" quavers one.

An oath explodes from another man, as he spits rudely on the floor. "Bah!" he growls. "He wanted us to leave this city—he says that God is going to destroy Sodom!"

The first man erupts into a high-pitched giggle. "So how does your father-in-law know what God intends to do?"

"Angels came to warn him—or so he says!"

The men erupt into coarse laughter. "Angels, huh? When is this destruction supposed to occur?"

"Enough!" roars one of the men. "I will not marry his daughter after all—it is a curse to have a crazy man for a relative! He will be leaving the city at daybreak tomorrow—and then we will be rid of him!"

Suddenly the eyes of one of the men light on you—and your flesh crawls as a menacing grin spreads slowly over his face.

"Look here, friends," he says. "What a beautiful youth for our evening's pleasure! Come here, you lovely creature!"

Horrified, you back slowly away—but all the men are on their feet now, their eyes glittering dangerously as they look at you. You back out of the doorway, honestly terrified now. *Why did I ever want to see this wicked place?* you think, looking desperately for a way to escape.

You are numb with fear when suddenly the clean white flames of the chariot envelop you, blocking the leering faces from sight.

"I feel filthy!" you sob miserably. "I wish I'd never come here!"

The steed's voice is calm. "Sin defiles, little one. The stench of the sin of the men of Sodom reaches even to Heaven."

Unhappily, you realize that you should have known better than to come here—for you remember that Lot's sons-in-law did not go with him when he escaped the city.

"You have no decision to make this time, my friend. I shall take you now to the destruction of Sodom, where you will see for yourself how the Lord hates that vile city!"

Dread and excitement mix uncomfortably in your heart as you take up the reins and wait.

Go to page 96.

(The Birth of Isaac)

Soft breezes fan the flap of the largest tent door as you find yourself once more in the settlement of Abraham. Sheep, goats, and cattle graze on the lush slopes; men and women cluster around this central tent, their faces expectant. A young woman pulls at your elbow insistently. "Does Abraham truly have a son?" she whispers.

Abraham himself suddenly appears at the door of his tent. His face wreathed in smiles, he holds aloft a tiny white bundle. Your jaw drops in amazement as you see a red, wrinkled face peeping from the mummy-like wrappings. *Those must be swaddling clothes!* you think in excitement. The baby is bound so snugly, he couldn't possibly wiggle. His tiny mouth opens wide, and he squalls furiously. Abraham beams with pride and the people clustered around the tent call out their congratulations.

"He shall be called Isaac," Abraham announces, and the crowd roars with laughter.

Irritated, you turn to the young woman at your side. "What's so funny?" you ask, puzzled that Abraham does not seem to be insulted.

A smile flits across her face. "The name Isaac means 'laughter'—both Abraham and Sarah laughed when the Lord told them that Sarah

would have a child in her old age! Their son's name will always remind them that the Lord can always do the impossible, even though we do not think it!"

You catch a glimpse of the leaping white flames of the chariot just behind the tent. In the general rejoicing, no one notices you slip away and climb in behind the steed.

"You may now decide between two events in the future," says the voice quietly. "You may see what happens because of the jealousy between Sarah and Hagar, or you may go to the time of Sarah's death. What is your decision?"

Wondering which might help you more on your quest, you take the cool reins in your hands, and decide.

If you decide to see the jealousy between Sarah and Hagar, go to page 106.

If you decide to go to Sarah's death, go to page 122.

(You Have Decided to See the Jealousy Between Sarah and Hagar)

"Come on!" shouts an excited voice in your ear. A boy about your age tugs urgently on your arm. "Have you *seen* all the food?"

Throngs of laughing people move up the slopes of the now-familiar hills near Hebron. You and your companion break into an easy run through wildflowers that dot the landscape as far as you can see. Beneath a massive oak tree in the distance, you see Abraham.

As you draw near, you see mountains of food heaped invitingly on skins spread on the grass. *It's a picnic!* you realize, and it looks like everyone has been invited. Bowls and platters are piled high with fruits, huge rounds of cheese, and flat breads, and the tantalizing aroma of roasting meat wafts through the air. Women cluster around stone hearths where soup bubbles in huge earthenware pots.

A little boy perches happily on Abraham's shoulders. You see Sarah nearby, watching her husband and son fondly. The little boy wiggles suddenly.

"Down!" he commands, his chubby little finger pointing imperiously.

Abraham laughingly scoops the little boy high in the air, then sets him gently on the ground. You watch in amusement as the toddler trots swiftly across the grass, his eyes fixed on a tempting plate of cakes.

Your companion eyes the little boy with a grin. "He doesn't care that this feast is in his honor— Isaac only cares about those cakes!" he laughs.

Suddenly a young man steps out from behind a tree. You recognize Ishmael, and are horrified at the jealous rage in his eyes as he looks at the toddler. Isaac's face is gleeful as he stretches his dimpled hand out for a cake—and in one swift motion, Ishmael whisks the platter away, holding it high over his head.

"Oh-oh," mutters your companion under his breath. Isaac's face crumples in disappointment, and tears fill his eyes. Ishmael sneers down at him, his taunting laugh almost a growl in his throat. Isaac backs away, for his half-brother's hatred is a sudden deadly presence. The little boy tumbles backward in his haste to get away, and he falls heavily.

Like a whirlwind, the still-beautiful Sarah rushes to her child, scooping him up swiftly. Tears streak Isaac's cheeks as he stares, uncomprehending, at his admired older brother. The platter of cakes falls to the ground as Ishmael defiantly faces Sarah. Hagar appears swiftly

behind her son, her eyes glittering with hatred and resentment.

In swift strides, Abraham reaches Sarah, who still cradles Isaac protectively. Her voice shaking with rage, Sarah commands, "Drive out this woman and her son, for the son of a slave *shall not* be an heir with my son Isaac!"

Abraham speaks softly in Sarah's ear, and leads her a short distance away.

"Whew!" murmurs your companion. "My mother said this was bound to happen sooner or later. It's too bad that Ishmael is so jealous that he can't see what's right in front of him! Abraham still loves him just as much as he ever has!"

Uncomfortable, you remember vividly the look you saw on Ishmael's face as he watched Isaac. "But it's no wonder that Ishmael is jealous," you protest feebly. "It doesn't seem fair that Isaac is to be Abraham's heir, when Ishmael is his son, too."

The boy stares at you. "Fair!" he replies. "Of course it is fair. The son of a slave woman is *never* the heir when a man has a son by his wife. Hagar has always known that her son would not be Abraham's heir—and she should never have encouraged Ishmael to think he would be!"

"But isn't Sarah being awfully harsh to want Hagar and Ishmael sent away?" you ask.

Your companion chuckles. "You wouldn't say so if you'd seen what Sarah had to put up with from Hagar for so many years! Besides, Hagar will be given her freedom eventually anyway—that's the custom. It is almost time for Ishmael to find a wife, and begin a family of his own—Sarah is wise to see that nothing but trouble can follow where such resentment exists. Come!" he continues as he turns eagerly toward the food. "I'm starving!"

You see the chariot of fire waiting on the crest of the hill; swiftly you make your way toward it and climb aboard. "Now you will be taken to the time of Sarah's death," says the steed.

Wait a minute! you think as you take up the reins. *When did Sarai's name change to Sarah?* You know that is not part of your quest, but you're curious just the same. Perhaps you will be able to find out.

Go to page 122.

(You Have Decided to See Hagar in the Wilderness the Second Time)

Endless dunes cover the land in every direction, bathed in pale moonlight. Scrubby desert vegetation clings stubbornly to life, silhouetted against the chalky, gray sand. The only movement or sound is that of the mournful wind, and you wonder what you are supposed to do. Suddenly, a wail of despair rends the air and you move instinctively toward the cry. The sand gives way beneath your feet and you tumble to the ground—sliding wildly down a dune that is still warm from sunshine long past.

Coming to a halt at last, you see the figure of a woman—her shoulders slumped in defeat, her face buried in her hands. She sobs noiselessly now, her body wracked with agony. Uncertain, you get to your feet—you are unwilling to intrude on her grief. The wind moans, carrying the desolation of the desert in its lonely cry.

Swiftly and terribly, total silence stills the wind. Your ears throb, and you see Hagar lift her tear-stained face heavenward. The black velvet curtain of night is torn by a dazzling flood of brilliance—you shield your eyes, for you are certain that you will be blinded if you do not.

"What is the matter with you, Hagar?" thunders a deep, mellow voice from above. "Do not fear, for God has heard the voice of the lad."

Shading your eyes with your forearm, you peer into the bushes of the ravine. Bathed in radiance, the straggly bushes cast sharp black shadows—and you see a young man lying crumpled, striped by the dark fingers of the shadows.

"Arise, lift up the lad," the rich voice tolls like an enormous, deep bell, "Hold him by the hand; for I will make a great nation of him."

As if in a dream, Hagar glides toward the lifeless-looking body of her son. Suddenly a startled, grateful cry erupts from her. She darts forward, snatching up a water bag—and the shimmering flames of the chariot engulf you.

"Will Ishmael live?" you ask nervously.

The sparkling voice of the steed is comforting as it answers, "Of course he will, little one. God has just now opened Hagar's eyes to show her a well—they were never out of the Lord's protection. Now," the voice continues, "I am allowed to take you back in time to the covenant between the Lord and Abram."

As you take the reins in hands trembling with excitement, you resolve to remember God's care of Hagar and Ishmael.

Go to page 69.

(You Have Decided to Stay With the Servants)

Light breezes rustle through thousands of quivering poplar leaves, sounding like hushed whispers of a vast congregation. A low mountain ridge runs from north to south, and gnarled and ancient olive trees cover the slopes thickly. Two figures toil up the mountain. One bears a load of wood upon his back, and the other holds a flaming torch. A voice breaks the stillness, and you turn to see two men sitting in the shade of a dense grove of olive trees. A donkey grazes contentedly nearby, and a sparkling stream rushes over silvery rocks.

"I just don't understand," says the younger of the two men, his voice uneasy. "Abraham took the torch, and the wood for the offering—but no animal to sacrifice."

The other one shakes his head, his eyes troubled. "Something's bothering Isaac, too. I thought he looked afraid, and he is not easily frightened. I've never seen him so pale."

"Still," says the younger man, "Abraham said that they would BOTH return. So if he is intending to . . ." his voice falters, " . . . to sacrifice his son—then he must know that the Lord God will bring Isaac back to life!"

What? you wonder, so startled that you almost exclaim out loud. *Abraham said that they would both return? Then he must have had complete faith in God's promises that were to be fulfilled in Isaac! Which means*, you think excitedly, *that Abraham fully expected God to raise his sacrificed son from the dead!*

You feel an overwhelming urge to follow Abraham and his beloved son, and you break into a jog up the foot of the low ridge. *Now* you understand why God required Abraham to sacrifice his son—each one of us must love God first and foremost, trusting in Him alone *by faith*. Abraham had already passed the test—because by faith he was trusting that God would fulfill His promises!

Heedless of the branches that tear at your face, you struggle up the slope, your mouth dry and your heart pounding. At last you halt, panting—for Abraham and his son have reached the summit not twenty feet away from you.

Go to page 115.

(You Have Come
   to the Place of Sacrifice)

Massive outcroppings of grey rock conceal you from the two figures a short distance away. Jolted, you realize that Isaac is not the little toddler you had thought—he appears to be about fifteen years old. Tall and sinewy, he removes the large bundle of firewood in one easy motion from his back. Abraham hands him the flaming torch, and busies himself building flattened rocks into a rough altar.

A few twisted trees cling to life on the rugged slopes of the ridge, and the wind sighs mournfully. Far below, where vegetation is much thicker, you see the two young servants. Time seems to stand still under the burning blue vault of sky, as you watch Abraham carefully pile the firewood on the top of the stone altar.

"My father!" says Isaac suddenly, breaking the silence. Abraham looks up from his work with a gentle smile—and pain-filled eyes. "Here I am, my son."

"Behold, the fire and the wood—but where is the lamb for the burnt offering?" questions Isaac, his face pale and still.

You realize that Isaac must have at least *suspected* that he was to be the sacrifice, for his father had brought no animal to the mountaintop. Amazed, you look at the face of the young man; Isaac is visibly afraid, yet has made no attempt to escape what he must sense is coming.

"God himself will provide the lamb for the burnt offering, my son," answers Abraham in a voice filled with dread and determination.

You watch in horror as Abraham begins to bind his son with a strong rope. Isaac stands ramrod straight with only a faint tremble in his hands and knees betraying his terror. As his father begins to guide him toward the altar, the young man's eyes flutter closed and his lips move soundlessly. Without a word from either of them, Abraham strains to lift his son onto the pile of wood. All of nature seems to hang suspended in deadly silence as Abraham pulls the knife from his belt and raises it high above his son. A shaft of light glints menacingly against the point of the cold, bronze blade.

"Abraham! ABRAHAM!" calls a deep and mighty voice.

Abraham lifts his grief-stricken face heavenward. "Here I am," he answers in awesome simplicity.

"DO NOT STRETCH OUT YOUR HAND AGAINST THE LAD. DO NOT DO ANYTHING TO HARM HIM. NOW I KNOW THAT YOU FEAR GOD, BECAUSE YOU HAVE NOT WITHHELD YOUR SON, YOUR ONLY

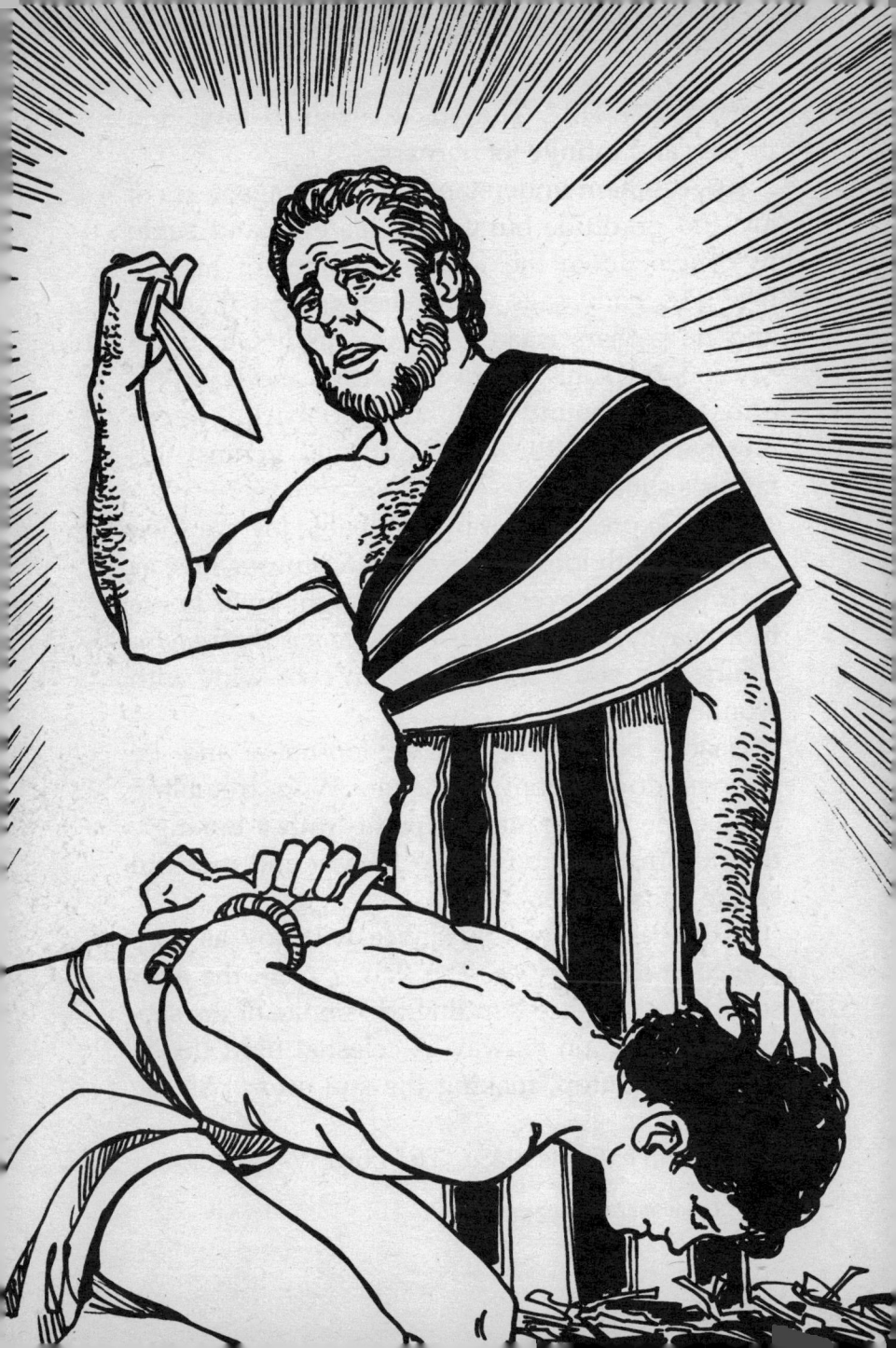

SON, FROM ME." The voice is full of love, and power, and infinite tenderness.

As Abraham understands the message, tears of joy and gratitude burst from his eyes and begin to course down the weathered lines of his old face. His body sags with relief against the alter and he gathers Isaac into his arms. "Oh, Isaac! My son, my son!" weeps the father, and Isaac, his arms still bound behind his back, weeps unashamedly with relief and joy against his father's shoulder.

Their expressions of indescribable joy are soon replaced with looks of awe and rapturous love as their tear-filled eyes see a ram caught by its horns in a nearby thicket. *That ram was not there just a minute ago,* you think, your own eyes wide with wonder.

Isaac's bonds are swiftly loosened and he springs down from the altar. With trembling hands, the young man helps his father untangle the ram from the bush, and a swift and merciful stroke ends its life.

Father and son fairly dance with joy as they conclude the sacrifice. The flames from the altar seem also to dance, sending the smoke of the sacrifice joyfully on its way. A celestial light floods the mountaintop, making the sun seem pale by comparison.

"We will call this place, 'The Lord Will Provide',"

Abraham tells his son. Suddenly, the feelings of love, joy, and gratitude that pass between father and son, as well as their determination to obey the Lord God Almighty in *all* things, seems too intensely personal for you to witness anymore. You drop your eyes just as the voice speaks again.

"I SWEAR BY MYSELF, THAT BECAUSE YOU HAVE DONE THIS AND HAVE NOT WITHHELD YOUR SON, YOUR ONLY SON, FROM ME, I WILL SURELY BLESS YOU, AND MAKE YOUR DESCENDANTS AS NUMEROUS AS THE STARS OF THE HEAVENS, AND AS THE SAND ON THE SEASHORE. YOUR DESCENDANTS WILL TAKE POSSESSION OF THE CITIES OF THEIR ENEMIES, AND THROUGH YOUR OFFSPRING ALL NATIONS ON EARTH WILL BE BLESSED, BECAUSE YOU HAVE OBEYED ME."

With your head still bowed, a sudden sense of grief overwhelms you as you remember another time when the Father *would* allow His only Son to be sacrificed!

"And that sacrifice will take place on this very hill," the voice of the steed says gently into your ear. As the flames of the chariot engulf you, your senses reel with the overpowering majesty of what you have just seen, and with new, profound understanding of obedience. *Abraham waited one hundred years for Isaac to be born,* you think, *and Isaac was evidently the only child that Sarah ever had.*

Abraham must have loved Isaac as much as any father can ever love his son, and yet he was going to kill him because God told him to. You condider this. *How does a person develop such an awesome reverence for God? When Jesus said that anyone who wanted to be His disciple must hate his own father and mother, did He mean that in comparison to our love for God, our love for our family must seem like hate?*

The questions tumbling around in your mind are interrupted by the voice of the steed. "Those are good questions, little one, and they reveal the beginning of wisdom. Perhaps on another quest, you can seek the answers to some of the teachings of Jesus. But on *this* quest, you have but one more stop. I shall take you now to a time some two thousand years after Abraham. You shall visit an early Christian church in Galatia, where the believers have just received a letter from the apostle Paul."

The heaviness in your heart is replaced by eager anticipation as you think, *Wow! This should be really interesting!* Eagerly you take up the reins.

Go to page 141.

(You Have Decided
to Go to Sarah's Death)

Gusts of wind tear at your tunic as you stand on the rocky summit of a ridge of low mountains. Far below, the Jordan River winds snake-like through lush green banks. Wildflowers dot the slopes, their brilliant colors flashing like gems. A large group of people moves up the incline toward the dark mouth of a cave cut into the rock. You see the figure of a woman stretched out upon a bier that is carried on the shoulders of four weeping men.

The procession enters the cave and the wind carries the mourners' wails to the very tops of the mountains. A muffled sob from nearby startles you and you whirl around to see a girl huddled against a rock, crying bitterly.

She wipes the tears from her face with the back of her hand as she sees you approach and jumps to her feet stammering, "I . . . d-d-did not think . . . I-I-I would be . . .m-m-missed . . ." she stutters painfully. You agonize for her as she struggles with each word.

Swiftly, you reassure her, "No, of course not. I just came up here to think."

Her eyes swim with tears in her plain little face. "It's j-j-just that . . . I w-w-will *m-m-miss* S-S-Sarah!" she sobs. "I never st-st-stammered . . . when I t-t-talked to her. Sh-sh-she was always p-p-patient and kind," the words begin to tumble out now. "She hoped in the Lord always; I l-l-loved being with her."

You realize with a jolt that before these journeys
began, you never thought about the people in the
Bible as *people*—they loved and were loved, they
laughed, they sorrowed, and they were missed
when they were gone.

"Could I ask you something?" you inquire softly.

"Of course," she answers shyly, her dark pansy
eyes still brimming with tears.

"Why was Sarai's name changed to Sarah?"

"Oh, that was s-s-so wonderful!" she exclaims.
"S-S-Sarah told me all about it! When the Lord c-c-
changed Abram's name to Abraham, He also
changed her name to Sarah, w-w-which means
'princess.' The Lord told Abraham that Sarah
would have a s-s-son and that she would be a
mother of nations," she continues, her eyes wide

with wonder. "God p-p-promised that kings of peoples would come from her. And then," she adds with a little trill of laughter, "Abraham and S-S-Sarah laughed!"

"Why did they laugh?" you wonder aloud.

The girl smiles broadly. "Because Sarah was ninety years old when God made the p-p-promise!

"I m-m-must go now," she smiles shyly. "And I think," she adds with a proud lift to her quivering little chin, "that I can honor S-S-Sarah by trying to hope in the Lord always, l-l-like she did!" She straightens her thin shoulders bravely, and moves down toward the cave.

The flames of the chariot engulf you, and the cave disappears. Thoughtfully, you take the smooth leather reins in your hands.

"Your choice now is between two events in the future," says the steed quietly. "You may go to the time of Abraham's death, or to see Abraham with his new wife, Keturah, after the death of his beloved Sarah."

If you decide
to go to Abraham's death, go to page 131.

If you decide to see Abraham with
Keturah, go to page 129.

(You Have Decided to See Rebekah Chosen)

You gasp as you find yourself perched on a narrow reed chair, pitching gently from side to side on a camel's back. The ground looks very far away, and you feel precariously balanced. Green mountains rise in the distance and a walled city shimmers in the heat. You see the beehive-shaped houses of brick outside the city walls and realize that you are approaching Haran.

A swift count shows you that ten camels, each heavily loaded with bulging skin bags, are hitched together in a line; a donkey far ahead leads the caravan. An old man walks beside the donkey, his hand resting affectionately on the animal's head. Drawing near the city, you hear voices raised in good-natured haggling as merchants barter with their customers.

Your heart leaps into your throat as your camel suddenly pitches forward and drops down on its front knees. Your fingers are clawing desperately for a secure hold when the rear end of the camel lowers just as swiftly. You glance quickly backward and see the rest of the camels doing the same thing—and no one seems to be falling off! At last, your camel drops all the way to the ground and you scramble hastily off.

The old man who led the caravan kneels stiffly on the ground, bows his silvery head, and lifts his hands in supplication.

"O Lord, the God of my master Abraham," he says softly, "please grant me success today, and show lovingkindness to my master Abraham. Behold, I am standing by the spring, and the daughters of the men of the city are coming out to draw water. Now may it be that the girl to whom I say, 'Please let down your jar so that I may drink,' and who answers 'Drink, and I will water your camels also,' may she be the one whom Thou hast appointed for Thy servant Isaac. And by this I shall know that Thou hast shown lovingkindness to my master."

His prayer finished, the old man clambers awkwardly to his feet and turns a smiling face toward you. His dark eyes twinkle as he says, "Now we will see what happens, my friend!" Together you watch a lovely young woman approach the well, balancing a huge jar easily on one shoulder. Carefully, she lowers her jar into the fountain, bringing it up brimming full. The old man limps quickly toward her. "Please let me drink a little water from your jar," he asks the girl gently.

"Drink, my lord," the girl says, quickly lowering her jar. Her smile is kind as she watches Abraham's old servant drink his fill. "I will draw also for your camels until they have finished drinking," she continues, her soft voice musical and soothing.

The old man straightens, watching her silently as she empties the contents of her jar into a nearby trough. The girl moves lightly back and forth from the well to the trough, until all the camels have been watered. At last she turns to Abraham's servant with a smile.

His old hands tremble slightly as he takes her hands and slides two intricately-molded golden bracelets upon her slender wrists. "Whose daughter are you?" the old man asks. "Please tell me, is there room for us to lodge in your father's house?"

The young woman smiles gently. "I am Rebekah, the daughter of Bethuel, the son of Milcah and Nahor. We have plenty of both straw and feed, and room to lodge in."

The old man bows low, his face radiant. "Blessed be the Lord, the God of my master Abraham, who has not forsaken His lovingkindness and His truth toward my master. As for me, the Lord has guided me in the way to the house of my master's brothers."

You remember now that Nahor was one of Abraham's brothers—so Rebekah must be his grandniece. The girl slips lightly away, as Abraham's servant reties the cords binding the camels.

Soon, a young man about the same age as Rebekah, hurries over to the old man. "Come in, blessed of the Lord!" he invites courteously. "Why do you stand outside since I have prepared the house, and a place for the camels?"

The old servant's glowing face disappears in the shining flames of the chariot. *Abraham was wise to let the Lord choose a wife for his son,* you reflect. *What a trusting, happy face she has.*

The familiar voice of the steed breaks gently into your thoughts. "Your quest is almost finished, little one. I shall take you back in time now, to a very solemn event—Abraham's preparation to sacrifice his only son, Isaac. You may choose to stay with his servants at the foot of the mountain, or you may choose to witness what happens at the scene of the sacrifice. Mark well what you learn at either place."

You feel unwilling to watch Abraham bind his little son to the altar—your blood runs cold at the very thought. You know which choice would make you less uncomfortable—but which would be the wisest?

If you decide to stay with the servants, go to page 113.

If you decide to go to the sacrifice, go to page 115.

(You Have Decided to See Abraham With Keturah)

You are standing in the shadow of Abraham's tent, in the familiar hills outside Hebron. Tents cover the landscape; cattle, sheep, and goats graze on the lush green grass from the crown of the hills to the winding Jordan River far below. Abraham, much older now, stands framed in the doorway of his huge tent. His eyes gaze dreamily at his vast domain; his face lights suddenly as the happy shouts of children at play reach him on the sweetly-scented spring air.

A young woman appears beside Abraham in the doorway.

"I hope that the Lord God will give me many children for you, my lord," she says with a shy smile.

Abraham pats her fondly. "He shall do as He wills, Keturah — we may safely leave the future in His hands."

You look at the grand old patriarch, whose features are serene and contented. Mountains of time seem to march before him: Isaac, Jacob, and Joseph, who would become the governor of all Egypt. Then slavery for the descendants of Abraham in a strange land, where they would groan in captivity until Moses came to set them free. Jacob would father Joseph as well as the line of Moses, you reflect in awe.

The peaceful countryside disappears in dancing light as you find yourself back in the chariot.

"You are right, little one," the steed says softly. "In Abraham are many nations. His union with Keturah will produce a son, Midian — the father of the Midianites, whose daughter will one day marry Moses. But now it is time for you to learn more. I am permitted to take you into the past, to learn about Abram's name change."

Go to page 81.

(Abraham's Death)

You find yourself in the cool shadow of a huge tent. A coarse curtain forms a partition, and in the room beyond you hear low voices. Rugs cover the ground and bulging sacks lean against the middle tent post. Quantities of skin bags hang from all the poles, and light flickers wanly from an oil lamp. A quick glance out the tent door shows you that night is falling, for shadows melt into darkness. A sharp wail from beyond the curtain makes your skin prickle uneasily.

Suddenly, the still evening air is filled with shrieks, followed by wails of grief. You watch in horrified fascination as several men and women erupt from behind the partition, tears flowing down their cheeks. The men tear desperately at their tunics, ripping them into tatters. Furiously, they beat their chests with clenched fists, while howls of grief erupt from their throats.

"Abraham has been gathered to his people," sobs one. Other wails begin outside as the news spreads that Abraham is dead. You feel oddly embarrassed by this way of expressing sorrow, for it is strange to you. The tent empties quickly, and the flames of the chariot surround you.

Relieved to be away from a scene you do not understand, you quickly pick up the reins.

"You find their mourning distasteful, my child?" asks the voice quietly.

"Well," you struggle for words that will not sound rude, "they are so dramatic, it almost seems disrespectful!" Silence follows, and embarrassment makes you flush unhappily. At last, the steed's gentle voice breaks the silence.

"You are a product of your culture, child. In your time, death and sorrow are denied — hidden away, covered over. Emotion is distrusted, and the intellect is worshiped; your culture believes that intellect is superior to emotion, and so emotion is denied. Is it not so?"

Surprised, you consider this carefully.

"These people do not prize intellect above all else. Life is often a difficult struggle, and they do not have the luxury of denying death. When they feel sorrow, they mourn — and when they feel joy, they rejoice. Now do you understand?"

Slowly, you begin to nod. Perhaps you can learn something about expressing emotion from this time in history.

"Now you will go back in time to learn about Abram's name change." *Great!* you think happily, remembering that at least part of your quest is to learn why his name was changed. *This should answer at least one question!*

Go to page 81

(You Have Decided to Go to the Birth of Jacob and Esau)

You find yourself among multitudes of tents once again; the sky is a blaze of pink and purple in the east as the sun peeps over the horizon. Shepherds on every hill call to their sheep and birds twitter as they soar skyward from their night's rest. An older woman sits cross-legged just outside a large tent, calmly turning a millstone to grind grain. A young servant girl helps her turn the heavy stone, and the sound—though not particularly musical—is somehow soothing.

"Run inside, child—you forgot the corn," says the woman quietly.

"Yes, Deborah," answers the girl with a smile. "I'm sorry I forgot. I was just so excited about Rebekah's twins!" Jumping to her feet, the girl hurries inside the tent.

"Would you like me to help you turn that?" you ask politely, as you approach the older woman.

Her kind eyes smile at you. "I thank you for your helpfulness young master," she replies softly, "but no. This is my work and my pleasure. I must stop grinding soon anyway to help my Rebekah with her new twins. Her task will be a difficult one," she says with a sigh.

You nod vigorously. "Twins must be twice as hard to take care of," you answer.

Deborah smiles gently. "Oh no, young master—it's not that. But she will need to be a very wise mother—that is the difficult task."

You look at her blankly. "Why will she need so much wisdom?"

The woman shifts her gaze faraway. "Because of the promise given to her boys. Much harm may come if she fails to guide them properly."

Bewildered, you question, "What do you mean?"

"The Lord our God has said that two nations were in Rebekah's womb, and that one would be stronger than the other—the older will serve the younger. Even in birth, the younger twin came forth with his hand grasping the heel of his older brother." The woman pauses, her face troubled. "Jealousy and strife will come between the brothers, unless Rebekah is very wise."

"But how can she change that," you puzzle, "since God has already said that the older will serve the younger? It doesn't seem very fair," you mutter.

"Fair?" the old woman smiles. "The Lord God chooses whom He will bless, and no one *deserves* His blessings, my son. Shall I resent the Lord because I was chosen to serve, and not to lead? Shall I rail against God because I am but a humble nurse, and not a queen? This is foolishness, young master. Rebekah *must* teach both her babies that the secret of righteousness lies in our willingness to do our Lord's bidding. Then there will be no strife and envy."

A lusty wail shatters the still morning, and Deborah turns into the tent with a smile. You find yourself back once more in the chariot of fire.

"Your choice now is between the future and the past," says the steed quietly. "You may go forward to see Jacob's name changed, or backward to see Rebekah chosen as Isaac's wife."

If you decide to see Jacob's name changed, go to page 136.

If you decide to see Rebekah chosen, go to page 125.

(You Have Decided to See Jacob's Name Changed)

As the leaping white flames curl around the chariot, you wonder how this choice could possibly help you learn what you must on your quest. After all, Jacob is Abraham's grandson! As you ponder, you notice that the flames are parting a bit, allowing you a glimpse of something below, rushing past at great speed. You lean eagerly over the side of the chariot to peer below.

Your heart leaps into your throat and your fingers tighten convulsively on the chariot, for the ground below is miles away. Tiny squares of fields rush beneath you like a checkerboard in motion, and clouds race swiftly over folds of mountains. With dizzying speed, the ground rushes to meet you; you shrink back against the side of the chariot.

"Where are you taking me?" you ask, your voice hollow.

"We go now to the river Jabbock," responds the steed. "Jacob will see Esau, his brother, face to face for the first time in more than twenty years. He is afraid, for he has not seen his brother since he deceived their father, Isaac, and received the blessing that rightfully belonged to Esau. Jacob ran for his life, and has not faced Esau since."

The shimmering flames part still wider, and you find yourself on the ground, surrounded by thickly-wooded hills. The sky to the east is ablaze with the ruddy-purple glow of dawn, and shadows are just beginning to melt into daylight. A silvery river slices through the green hills. On the opposite bank, you see two men wrestling desperately on the grass.

Surprised to find that you are still inside the chariot, you ask, "Is that Jacob? Who is the other man?"

The steed's voice is low and reverent, bell-like in the velvety silence of dawn. "Jacob wrestles with the Lord, little one."

A deep voice, piercing you to your very core, breaks the silence. This voice could create or destroy, and you tremble at the sound.

"Your name shall no longer be Jacob," says the voice, "but Israel; for you have striven with God and with men and have prevailed."

Flames engulf you once more, and the two figures fade. "I don't understand," you protest. "Why would the Lord wrestle with Jacob? And why did He change Jacob's name?"

"Have you never struggled, little one—only to find at last that you must rely *only* on the Lord?" The steed's voice is gentle as it continues. "Jacob, in his pride, tried to steal by trickery what God had already promised him. But Jacob has learned,

in this last twenty years, that he is unworthy of the Lord's lovingkindness and faithfulness; he has at last learned to rely on the Lord, and not on his own scheming devices."

"But," you stammer, "I still don't understand."

"When Jacob knew that he wrestled with the Lord, he also knew that he could never win—that his own struggles and scheming could never prevail against his maker. At last he gave up his own pride, and simply hung onto the Lord—asking for His blessing. And because Jacob's heart had changed, the Lord changed his name from 'he deceives' to 'he struggles with God'."

At last you understand what has puzzled you every time you have read the story. "I think I see!" you begin eagerly. "The changed *name* was important because Jacob's *heart* had changed— that's why God changed his name!"

"Exactly!" answers the steed, its joyful laugh chiming like a thousand sparkling prisms. "Now I will take you back to Mount Moriah, where Abraham is preparing to sacrifice Isaac."

Your scalp prickles uneasily. "I really don't understand that," you say haltingly. "Why did Abraham ever even *think* of slaughtering his only son?"

"Because the Lord God told Abraham to do so," replies the voice. You shudder, and without thinking you explode, "But that is so bloodthirsty!"

Silence greets your remark and swells until the blood pounding in your head makes your ears roar.

The steed's voice tolls like a deep bell, "Are you forgetting that the Lord God is the creator and giver of all life—and that because everything belongs to Him, He can do whatever He wishes? And are you forgetting that He did not ask Abraham to do anything that God would not require of himself?

Miserably you think of the sacrifice that God *would* make—for all those who doubt His love as you have just doubted.

"Your choice is this," interrupts the steed with infinite gentleness. "You will go back in time to Mount Moriah, where you may choose to stay with Abraham's servants at the foot of the mountain, or you may go to the place of sacrifice.

You think carefully and make your decision.

If you decide to stay with the servants, go to page 113.

If you decide to go to the place of sacrifice, go to page 115.

(Galatia, In Asia Minor)

You find yourself standing in the shadows of a brick-paved courtyard. Water splashes softly from a small stone fountain in the middle, and flowering vines spill from high grey walls. Several young children play quietly in the corner, while their parents cluster eagerly around an older woman seated on a low stone bench. Carefully, she rolls up a long strip of parchment, placing it tenderly on the bench beside her.

"Now do you see, my friends?" she asks smilingly. "We must stop trying to become Jews, for our own dear Paul has told us that Jewish law was a tutor to *lead us to Christ*—now we may be justified by faith." She rises to her feet, her face earnest. "Now that faith has come, we are no longer under a tutor. We are all children of God through faith in Christ Jesus—there is neither Jew nor Greek, there is neither slave nor free man, there is neither male nor female, for we are all one in Christ Jesus."

A young man frowns heavily. "I still don't understand, Drusilla," he says slowly. "How are the *Gentiles* sons of Abraham?"

Electrified, you remember that you must learn why Abraham's name change to "father of many" is important to us today. You cross the courtyard in swift strides, eager to hear the answer.

Drusilla smiles. "This is what Paul has written," she explains seriously. "Abraham believed God, and *because of his faith*, God accepted him as righteous. Abraham lived *before* the law was given by God through Moses, so he did not—could not—achieve righteousness through the law. And he certainly lived long before God sent His Son Jesus to pay the penalty for all sin, so Abraham was not found righteous because of Jesus. No, God told Abraham that all nations would be blessed through him. Abraham believed God, was blessed, and so all who believe are blessed as he was."

"Oh!" you exclaim suddenly, as understanding floods your mind. "If we believe in Christ Jesus by faith, we are Abraham's children—because Abraham is the father of all the faithful who believe!"

"Exactly!" replies Drusilla, her lined face breaking into a delighted smile "Christ redeemed us from the curse of the law, so that the blessing promised to Abraham might also be given to the Gentiles. Because of Christ, everyone may receive the Spirit promised by God. The promises were given to Abraham and to his 'seed.' God does not say, 'and to seeds,' as referring to many, but rather to one, 'and to your seed,' that is, Christ."

"Wait a minute, though," you begin hesitantly. "Does that mean that God's promises to Israel don't apply anymore? Are Christians the new chosen people?"

"My son," Drusilla speaks softly, "The Lord God does not break promises. His promises to Israel will be fulfilled, just as Scripture predicts in Deuteronomy, Nehemiah, Psalms, Isaiah, Jeremiah, Ezekiel, Zephaniah, and more. There will be a day when the Jews will look on Him whom they have pierced, and they will mourn, and they will believe."

The happy, contented faces fade from sight as you find yourself for the last time in the chariot of fire. For a brief moment you see the ages roll past like huge waves on an eternal sea—Abraham, Joseph, Moses, David: all individual lives pointing to the One who would save us all. You bid a silent farewell to Abraham, the father of the faithful, and prepare for home.

THE END